Improving the Quality

of Teaching Through

National Board Certification

Improving the Quality of Teaching Through National Board Certification

Jill Harrison Berg, NBCT

with foreword by James A. Kelly,
founding president of the National Board for Professional Teaching Standards

Contributing NBCTs

Jane Beane	Mary Guerino
Al Bird	Kevin Hart
Martha Bosco	Paul Lyness
Judith Cournoyer	Elizabeth Sales
Matthew Delaney	Carol Shestok
Jim Dixon	Anne Stacy

Christopher-Gordon Publishers, Inc.

Norwood, Massachusetts

Credits

Every effort has been made to contact copyright holders for permission to reproduce borrowed material where necessary. We apologize for any oversights and would be happy to rectify them in future printings.

Mission Statement reprinted with permission from the National Board for Professional Teaching Standards, www.nbpts.org. All rights reserved.

Five Core Propositions reprinted with permission from the National Board for Professional Teaching Standards, www.nbpts.org. All rights reserved.

Summary of the Evidence reprinted with permission from the National Board for Professional Teaching Standards, www.nbpts.org/research/archive. All rights reserved.

Testimonials reprinted with permission from the National Board for Professional Teaching Standards, *The Professional Standard*, Volume 1-#3 and #4, Volume 2-#2 and #4. All rights reserved.

Reading and Understanding Directions adapted with permission from the National Board for Professional Teaching Standards, Facilitator's Institute, July 1999. All rights reserved.

Material reprinted and adapted from the National Board Certification Candidate Support Resource Binder reprinted with permission from The Commonwealth of Massachusetts Department of Education.

Artwork created by Althea Zemnaan Berg and Summer Lee Martin Payton reprinted with permission of the artists.

The author thanks the National Board for Professional Teaching Standards its assistance. The assistance of the National Board in providing permission and checking accuracy in no way constitutes an endorsement of this book. The author is not affiliated with, nor does she represent in any manner, the National Board for Professional Teaching Standards, Inc. The designations "National Board Certified Teachers" and "National Board Certification" are awarded solely by the National Board. The phrases "National Board Certification" and "National Board Certified Teacher" are federally registered trademarks of the National Board.

Christopher-Gordon Publishers, Inc.
1502 Providence Highway, Suite #12
Norwood, Massachusetts 02062
800-934-8322
781-762-5577

Printed in the United States of America
10 9 8 7 6 5 4 3 2 1   07 06 05 04 03

ISBN: 1-929024-56-8
Library of Congress Catalogue Number: 2003101602

for Marylyn A. Harrison

and

Roger Scott Harrison, Jr.

my first teachers

Table of Contents

Preface

In 1998, the Massachusetts Commissioner of Education, David P. Driscoll, announced a new "Framework for Strengthening Massachusetts' Future Teaching Force." This framework, known as the 12-62 Plan, acknowledged that teachers are the most important factor in student achievement and aimed to improve educator quality in the Commonwealth. To this end, the commissioner called for a corps of 1000 Master Teachers by the year 2003. He established legislation that would strengthen teaching by initiating incentives and supports for teachers to work toward National Board Certification, then tap that capacity by encouraging those teachers to mentor new teachers or engage in new roles.

One of the most important and effective forms of support that the department offered to National Board Certification® candidates was coordinating Candidate Support Seminars. Held at locations throughout the state, these support seminars were led by National Board Certified Teachers® (NBCTs) who agreed to assist candidates by providing logistical, intellectual, technical, and emotional support. I served as one of those support facilitators using my own experiences with the certification process and teaching to assist candidates.

In order to support one another to be more effective, several candidate support facilitators began meeting in 1999. We described many similar experiences: witnessing candidates' first recognition of the real magnitude of the task, wrestling with how much to assist candidates with their writing, and deciding how to help candidates in making their own good choices in portfolio development. We also noted that groups of candidates, like the cohorts of children we teach, have their own character and needs. Some require coaching with their writing, others need to be supported for organization and time management, still others benefit most from sharing and reflecting together on videotapes of their teaching.

As I listened to these conversations, it became clear to me that some groups had found effective ways to build thoughtful conversations about teaching and learning out of the evidence being collected. Some groups turned their regular meetings into opportunities to engage in collective problem-solving, grounded in the student samples brought forward. Some groups took time to challenge one another's evidence choices, to examine exposed assumptions, and to confront inconsistencies in espoused theory and practice. The members of these groups would invariably discover that they had developed an increased ability to improve the quality of their teaching. I realized that while support facilitators would always need to consider what is best for "these candidates, at this time, in this setting," there could be a collection of best practices—a repertoire of support seminar activities from which these support facilitators might draw—which would allow those candidates to take fullest advantage of the professional development experience the National Board Certification process offers.

In the fall of 2000 I began to document the strategies the NBCT candidate support facilitators were using and during the spring of 2001 I met with a core of 12 dedicated support facilitators to discuss the activities and to compile them into a collection worth sharing. The Massachusetts Department of Education provided a copy of this collection to candidate support facilitators throughout Massachusetts in September 2001. Those candidate support facilitators experimented with the strategies in the collection, added ideas, and noted changes throughout the 2001–2002 candidate cycle.

At the same time, I received a fellowship to study at Harvard University's Graduate School of Education. I was drawn to understand more about teacher improvement and school reform efforts. I began to review the literature about professional development, learning groups, and adult learning. I was able to make important connections between these bodies of research and the work of our candidate support seminars. I began to understand why and how National Board Certification holds great promise to improve the quality of teaching. And I recognized that this information would be a valuable resource for a variety of educational stakeholders:

- It would give teachers who want to improve their teaching a clear understanding of why and how National Board Certification can help them to do so. It would help them understand the nature of the challenge and the purpose of National Board Certification. It would also provide them with practical strategies to support their growth during their candidacy.

- It would provide a knowledge base to inform the work of NBCTs (National Board Certified Teachers) and others who support National Board Certification candidates. It would also provide practical strategies for NBCTs who are eager to make an impact on the quality of teaching beyond their own classrooms.

- It would provide administrators, union leaders, and policy makers with an understanding of how National Board Certification can help them to build the capacity they need to enable other education reforms to be effective. And it would make clear to them the role they must play.

- It would help teacher preparation program directors who are concerned about the quality of the teachers their programs produce to see the important role that the professional standards set by the National Board should play in their programs. It would have practical implications for their efforts to recruit and retain quality teachers.

- It would even help educational researchers who want to make an impact on classroom teaching and student learning to recognize National Board Certified Teachers as valuable collaborators in their work.

I made a variety of difficult choices as I tried to address the varied interests of this broad audience. I had to determine whether to write this from my perspective as a practice-based researcher or a research-based practitioner. I decided to uphold the rigor and conventions of my research training without giving up the passion that comes from my experience with practice. I have placed citations at the end of each chapter to make the text more readable, and I have elected to include children's illustrations as a reminder that this book is really about serving children.

Most importantly, I had to make a decision about the presentation of this material. I felt it was important to not only provide practical strategies about how National Board Certification can improve the quality of teaching but to provide the research and theoretical framework that informs those strategies. Rather than weaving these two pieces together, I have framed this volume in two parts: theory and practice. I recognize that some readers will read these chapters in order, while others will undoubtedly jump to the practical suggestions in Part II before coming back to the theory in Part I.

Part I draws from research on effective professional development, group learning, and transformational adult learning in order to explain why National Board Certification should improve the quality of teaching and to articulate the conditions under which the National Board Certification experience provides the greatest benefit to both the individual teacher, through his/her practice, and to the collective good, through teaching culture.

Part II is a practical guide for improving the quality of teaching. The first section contains a toolkit that helps candidate groups know how to improve the quality of their teaching. This collection of practices, which has been developed and tested by 12 veteran candidate support facilitators, is supported by the research provided in Part I. It is organized by "strands" in order that candidates can easily identify the activities that will meet their needs. The second section of Part II contains practical advice for life after candidacy. It aims to educate NBCTs and other educational stakeholders about what they can do to increase the impact NBCTs are making beyond their own classrooms.

Four appendices are provided as resources. Appendix A provides a sampling of research studies and testimonials that support the claim that

National Board Certification is having an impact on teaching culture and on individual teachers' practice. It is clear that research in this area has only just begun. Appendix B provides a summary of the efforts of various stakeholders to improve the quality of teaching. Readers may find this to be an enlightening overview of current efforts to improve the quality of teaching, and the often unexamined assumptions which underlie them. NBCTs are well positioned and well prepared to play a role in enabling many of these efforts. Appendix C provides guidance on using videotapes as evidence of teaching and learning. The videotape-based entries of the National Board Certification portfolio can be a source of great anxiety for many teachers; this need not be the case. Candidates may want to provide a copy of this section to those who agree to assist them with the taping. Appendix D provides a list of Web-based professional resources. Candidates, group facilitators, and NBCTs will find these professional and logistical resources useful throughout candidacy as they seek to connect with education's knowledge base, as well as after candidacy as they seek to connect with new roles.

Acknowledgments

In 1997 my principal casually suggested that I consider pursuing National Board Certification. An intelligent academic, a visionary leader, and a model principal of the Cambridgeport School, Lynn Stuart must have known that National Board Certification would cause fundamental changes in my teaching practice, it would spread through the school and change the conversations teachers were having (five more teachers became involved within four years), and it would build the capacity among her staff that she would need to accomplish other goals (successful collaborations with research, strong relationships of trust with parents, and training and retention of new teachers.) But I doubt that she could have predicted that it would lead to a book with her name at the front of it. For initiating the series of events that have led to this book, I am truly indebted to Lynn Stuart.

There are many more Cambridgeport School colleagues whose support, friendship, and feedback have influenced my personal and professional experience with National Board Certification candidacy and support. Dan Monahan, Sarah Zevey Steinitz, Sarah Fiarman, Frederick Won Park, and Bela Bhasin are paramount among this group of critical friends. I also benefited during my own candidacy year from the encouraging words of NBCT advocate Joanna Cole and others whom I knew only via e-mail.

Cambridge Public Schools Superintendent Bobbie D'Allessandro and Director of Professional Development Valerie Spriggs recognized my accomplishment and knew that National Board Certification could have a role to play in improving the quality of teaching in the district. They supported me to establish a candidate support seminar for local teachers which has given me the opportunity to work closely with 30 candidates. This experience was not only rewarding, but it was vital to the development of this book. Thanks to Bobbie, Valerie, and all of these candidates, most of whom are now National Board Certified Teachers.

My candidate support work in Cambridge led to a consulting position at the Massachusetts Department of Education in which I helped to coordinate candidate support across the state as well as to pursue other National

Board-related initiatives. I enjoyed working with Mieka Freund, Elizabeth Pauley, Kristin LaMonica, and Meg Mayo-Brown on these projects. In particular, their support of my efforts to create the "Candidate Support Resource Binder" helped to ensure that the activities it contained would truly be useful. The binder benefited from the input of many people, but I must specifically acknowledge the dedication of the contributing authors who participated in numerous meetings to assess candidate learning needs, to develop, pilot and reflect on the binder, and improve it for inclusion in this book. They are Jane Beane, Al Bird, Martha Bosco, Judith Cournoyer, Matthew Delaney, Jim Dixon, Mary Guerino, Kevin Hart, Paul Lyness, Elizabeth Sales, Carol Shestok, and Anne Stacy. Tom Daniels and Mary Ellen Dakin also made important contributions in the first round of this work.

The experience of working with this candidate support cohort together with the experience of having engaging conversations with National Board Certified Teachers at local and national conferences led me to develop some hypotheses about how and why National Board Certification seemed to do what it did. I am grateful to the National Board for Professional Teaching Standards for providing these regular and rejuvenating opportunities for engagement through the annual conferences, the Facilitators' Institutes, and the National Invitational Research Conference. And I am grateful to good friends at the National Board, including Kathy Swann and Marlene Henriques, whose feedback on the manuscript helped me to make sure that it accurately represented the Board's work.[1]

I was lucky to have the opportunity to investigate my developing hypotheses further as a doctoral fellow at the Harvard University Graduate School of Education. With my advisor Steve Seidel behind me always asking the right questions, I have been able to expand my thinking in numerous ways. Professors such as Richard Elmore, Katherine Merseth, Susan Moore Johnson, Wendy Lutrell, and Robert Kegan guided me to relevant research, baited me to argue my ideas, challenged me to examine my assumptions, and supported me to take my ideas to a larger audience. Several of the ideas presented in this book sprang from course assignments and will undoubtedly continue to be central to my future research. I also feel lucky to have encountered at Harvard a cohort of wonderfully supportive and sharply insightful doctoral student colleagues. I have thrived on their encouragement throughout this project.

Of those who have encouraged me along the way, not all of them are aware of how inspiring and relevant to this work I have found their words and their example. Deborah Meier and Sharon Robinson shine for me as examples of strong, intelligent women who speak clearly and directly about the fundamental problems of our American education system; they maintain the rigor of research while speaking with the passion of practice in a way that I find inspiring. James Kelly went beyond my request for assistance on this project and offered wise and humorous stories from his personal and professional life that were full lessons for my own life and work.

My two grandmothers, both New York City Public School teachers, each spoke through a lifetime of deeds about the importance of having concern for other people's children; this same concern fuels my work and my passion for taking a systemic approach to improving the quality of teaching. This book is evidence of their legacy.

My family is at once my foundation and my inspiration. Limitless gratitude goes to my husband Erik who recognized how important this was to me before I saw it myself and supported me in numerous ways throughout the development of this project, my daughter Althea who always seemed to know when to leave me tiny love notes, my son Maceo who dutifully distracted me at regular intervals from writing this book which kept me sane, and my sister Rhonda who recently performed the miracle of birth and reminded me what it is all for. And finally, I owe the largest debt of gratitude to my parents, Roger and Marylyn Harrison, my first teachers, who taught me to know and love God and trained me to have the knowledge, skills and disposition to be of service to humanity.

Notes

1. The assistance of the National Board for Professional Teaching Standards in providing permission and checking accuracy in no way constitutes an endorsement of this book. The author is not affiliated with, nor does she represent in any manner, the National Board for Professional Teaching Standards, Inc.

Foreword

In the past 20 years, the vast school system in the United States has experienced intense pressure to improve student learning. Beginning in the late 1980's and continuing in the first years of the new century, the principal goal of education policy and reform has been to improve the educational attainment of all students, especially low performing students. These efforts came to be known as the "standards movement", and were led by coalitions of state governors, corporate leaders, and education reformers. Educators from all subject matter fields worked to produce statements of what students should be expected to learn and be able to do. The standards were spelled out for grade levels from first grade through high school graduation. The work was conducted separately within each field. State-level efforts followed, and within a few years, standards were ubiquitous.

Soon standards led to student testing, sometimes based on the new standards but, believe it or not, frequently not directly based on the academic content called for in the standards. Testing led to more testing, and then still more testing – all in the name of accountability, or rather, information about average student achievement.

Largely absent from this activity was attention to three critically important policy issues that must be addressed if significant and lasting change is to be realized. First, the basic organizational structure of the enterprise, the individual school, has exhibited impressive stability over the past century. While schools successfully adapted to sweeping demographic and social changes over the decades, they also resisted efforts to relax traditional bureaucratic structures and move to more professional forms of organization in which colleagues cooperate to improve the quality of their teaching. In fact, most schools today are organized pretty much the same way they were organized in the 1920's. Second, reformers paid scant attention to school curricula themselves – both what was supposed to be taught, and what was actually taught – and educators know that these are not always the same thing. Third, issues about the capacity of teachers and the quality of teaching were also overlooked.

An exception to this generalization was and is the National Board for Professional Teaching Standards (NBPTS), the organization that established and operates National Board Certification (NBC), a voluntary, advanced system of professional certification for accomplished teachers. (As that organization's founding president, and its chief executive for 12 years, the reader would both expect me to know something about NBPTS and NBC and also be forewarned about potential bias in my comments. But it undoubtedly was my involvement in creating the NBPTS and its NBC that led Jill Harrison Berg, herself deeply knowledgeable about both, to ask that I produce this Forward for her book.)

Jill Harrison Berg's thesis that teacher collaboration and collective learning are powerful pathways to improve teaching is a direct outgrowth of the methods used by the National Board to build and operate the system of National Board Certification. A majority of the members of the 63-member NBPTS board of directors are classroom teachers. From the beginning, the board enlisted in its work leaders from all parts of the educational enterprise, but insisted that practicing classroom teachers play central roles in every aspect of program development and organizational governance.

The work to build the NBC system was done in stages, each defined by the substantive task that was to be accomplished. First, the NBPTS developed and published "What Teachers Should Know and Be Able to Do", the unifying substantive statement already reshaping the professional landscape of the teaching profession. Released in 1989, this document quickly became one of the most influential documents published about teaching in the last half of the 20th century. Next came a "Framework for Certificates", defining the some-25 fields in which Certification is offered. (This number can be contrasted to the 1700 different named state licenses for teachers then offered by the 50 states; these 1700 licenses represented an overly specialized hodge-podge devoid of any reasonable professional or intellectual differentiation and content.) For each of the 25 fields in NBC, standards, and then groundbreaking performance assessments, were developed, requiring the invention of new organizational methods and professional and technical content at every step.

Policymakers from school boards to corporate boardrooms, from teacher unions to teaching specialty and disciplinary groups, instituted changes, some unprecedented, in public policies and institutional arrangements.

- High and rigorous standards for what accomplished teachers should know and be able to do are an accepted reality for the first time in American history.

- Performance assessments of teaching, once believed impossible to develop, are in use, measuring performance against written standards.

- Accepted as fair, reliable and valid, NBC standards-based assessments are in fact the best developed by any profession, and have never once even been challenged in a lawsuit.

- NBC provides teachers, teacher educators, and other educators with a powerful professional development "curriculum", especially in the portfolio component of the assessment process.

- Policymakers, union leaders, school administrators, school boards, governors of both parties, and corporate supporters have instituted financial incentives and increased compensation and recognition for National Board Certified Teachers (NBCTs) in over 40 states.

- NBPTS is now approaching the goal that every eligible teacher in America will be offered financial incentives to seek NBC and will be recognized and rewarded for achieving it.

- Teacher acceptance of NBC is widespread, reflecting their trust in an organization controlled by classroom teachers, and their confidence in the professional validity and fairness of an assessment process in which all assessors who evaluate candidate performances are teachers from the same specialty field as the candidate.

Throughout this remarkable development process, teachers were centrally involved at every stage. Teachers controlled the process, using the wisdom of their professional practice to guide and oversee the work of professors, assessment experts and political advisors alike – and I should add, to guide and oversee the work of the NBPTS staff and its president! In short, the NBPTS trusted teachers, and teachers learned to trust NBC.

Now NBPTS is working to "grow" the program to true national scale. There are now about 23,000 National Board Certified Teachers, and about the same number are candidates in the 2002-03 school year. Within ten years, it is reasonable to expect that the number of NBCTs will have grown to more than 200,000 teachers, and in 20 years, the number is likely to be closer to 300,000, or about 10% of the teacher workforce.

Teachers are involved in the NBC process as NBCTs, as candidates, as assessors, as coaches and mentors of candidates, and as policy advocates. As such, they face two challenges in the years ahead. Jill Harrison Berg addresses both of them in her book.

The first is that they must assure that other teachers, administrators and teacher educators understand the robust conceptions of teaching and learning that are embedded in the student learning parts of the assessment portfolios. These conceptions are rich in setting forth the knowledge of subject content, the understanding of student conditions and in the repertoire of accomplished teaching. They must insist that critics have read the standards and understand the content and methods of the assessments. By doing this they will assure that the NBC program remain a catalyst for powerful teacher learning, professional growth and student learning.

The second challenge grows out of the first. Leaders of NBPTS and its thousands of constituents must think and act more imaginatively, and with more courage, about how teaching and learning can be dramatically rethought and reformed to create effective and equitable 21st century learning opportunities for all children. The tradition of top-down, command-and-control school structures are dysfunctional because authority and control are not dominant needs of the organization today. Instead, schools of the future will feature decentralized and flexible opportunities for accomplished teachers to work with parents in the design of learning opportunities for all students. To create these learning opportunities, accomplished teachers must be leaders in the creation of new schools and the reform of existing schools. Accomplished teachers must learn to think like entrepreneurs creating new firms to provide more effective services in the marketplace for teaching and learning. These teachers will increasingly use the Internet to share their problems, their experiences and their video records of their performances, serving as critics for the work of colleagues, and using the standards and performance protocols of their emerging profession to achieve the goals for student learning established by school authorities.

In short, the professional vision of accomplished teaching, reflected in the standards and assessments of NBC, is only half the agenda. Leaders of the movement for accomplished teaching must urgently become directly engaged in educational policy and organizational reforms, so that the potential impact of accomplished teaching can be more fully and equitably realized in the lives of students.

Jill Harrison Berg is already such a teacher/leader. Herself a National Board Certified Teacher, she coaches and mentors candidates for NBC. She works collaboratively with other coaches and mentors to assist candidates in the development of their best possible assessment performances. In this book she offers theoretical perspectives on why accomplished teaching is effective and how teachers can work together to improve the teaching capacity and performance of each. She has collected and codified the professional wisdom of fellow coaches and mentors in the NBC process so that candidates and others can benefit from the disciplined professional development experience that is the essence of National Board Certification. She writes to prod other teacher-leaders to break out of old structures and roles and to become genuine leaders in working with other teachers to improve their teaching. She understands that National Board Certification is a journey, not a destination, that the effort to improve one's own teaching is a career-long process, and that teachers collaborating to help each other improve can help large numbers of teachers more ahead in their professional journey towards improved effectiveness.

This book will be useful not only to candidates for National Board Certification but to all teachers seeking to improve their practice. It will be useful to school administrators wishing to empower teachers to take responsibility to improve their teaching. It will be useful to teacher educators and others now engaged in professional development because it will help them focus on the learning of the teachers they are trying to help instead of the delivery of pre-conceived programs telling them what they should be doing. It will be useful to persons interested in advancing student learning and willing to consider methods to achieve it other than simply to require more and more student testing. Finally, the book will be fascinating to teachers wanting to improve but frustrated by ever-increasing top-down direction about one-size-fits-all pedagogy. In short, this book will contribute to efforts by many to build a more effective teaching profession, one empowered by large amounts of collegial interaction and professional cooperation.

James A. Kelly
January 26, 3003

Introduction

In 1986 the Carnegie Forum on Education and the Economy's Task Force on Teaching as a Profession responded to *A Nation at Risk* with *A Nation Prepared*, a report which called for the establishment of a National Board for Professional Teaching Standards. Within 1 year, the task force appointed a 63-member board dominated by classroom teachers to begin this work. The mission of this Board was ambitious but clearly defined, and the Board began its work by crafting a seminal document, *What Teachers Should Know and Be Able To Do*.[1] (See Figure 0.1.) This document, which essentially defines the profession by outlining Five Core Propositions of quality teaching, has initiated a new dialogue among teachers, among administrators, and between the two groups. It has led to the elaboration of "accomplished teaching standards" and a voluntary certification process that identifies teachers who are able to practice at the level of these standards. It has also led to the redesign of initial licensure regulations set by INTASC (Interstate New Teacher Assessment and Support Consortium) and the teacher education program accreditation process established by NCATE (National Council for Accreditation of Teacher Education). These Core Propositions are increasingly being incorporated into teacher quality initiatives at all stages of the teaching continuum. They have become the industry standard for the education profession. (See Figure 0.2.)

Figure 0.1: The NBPTS mission

The National Board's mission is to advance the quality of teaching and learning by:

- Maintaining high and rigorous standards for what accomplished teachers should know and be able to do

- Providing a national voluntary system certifying teachers who meet these standards

- Advocating related education reforms to integrate National Board Certification in American education and to capitalize on the expertise of National Board Certified Teachers

---

Reprinted with permission from the National Board for Professional Teaching Standards, www.nbpts.org, Mission Statement. All rights reserved.

What does the establishment of an industry standard for quality teaching have to do with improved teaching and learning? For decades teachers have been asked, begged, threatened, bribed, and cajoled to become better teachers. They have been paraded through workshops, conferences, and coursework. They have been introduced to a myriad of new strategies that they might try (or might not), and they have been tested and evaluated. Whereas each of these tactics may serve to increase teachers' knowledge and skill in some way, the big picture has remained unclear. Teachers had not been told exactly what good teaching is. No one had yet spelled out a clear benchmark for quality teaching that teachers might work to achieve.

Figure 0.2: The Five Core Propositions

The National Board for Professional Teaching Standards seeks to identify and recognize teachers who effectively enhance student learning and demonstrate the high level of knowledge, skills, abilities, and commitments reflected in the following **Five Core Propositions**.

1. **Teachers are committed to students and their learning.**

    Accomplished teachers are dedicated to making knowledge accessible to all students. They act on the belief that all students can learn. They treat students equitably, recognizing the individual differences that distinguish one student from another and taking account of these differences in their practice. They adjust their practice based on observation and knowledge of their students' interests, abilities, skills, knowledge, family circumstances and peer relationships.

    Accomplished teachers understand how students develop and learn. They incorporate the prevailing theories of cognition and intelligence in their practice. They are aware of the influence of context and culture on behavior. They develop students' cognitive capacity and their respect for learning. Equally important, they foster students' self-esteem, motivation, character, civic responsibility and their respect for individual, cultural, religious and racial differences.

2. **Teachers know the subjects they teach and how to teach those subjects to students.**

    Accomplished teachers have a rich understanding of the subject(s) they teach and appreciate how knowledge in their subject is created, organized, linked to other disciplines and applied to real-world settings. While faithfully representing the collective wisdom of our culture and upholding the value of disciplinary knowledge, they also develop the critical and analytical capacities of their students.

    Accomplished teachers command specialized knowledge of how to convey and reveal subject matter to students. They are aware of the preconceptions and background knowledge that students typically bring to each subject and of strategies and instructional materials that can be of assistance. They understand where difficulties are likely to arise and modify their practice accordingly. Their instructional repertoire allows them to create multiple paths to the subjects they teach, and they are adept at teaching students how to pose and solve their own problems.

cont.

3. **Teachers are responsible for managing and monitoring student learning.** Accomplished teachers create, enrich, maintain and alter instructional settings to capture and sustain the interest of their students and to make the most effective use of time. They also are adept at engaging students and adults to assist their teaching and at enlisting their colleagues' knowledge and expertise to complement their own. Accomplished teachers command a range of generic instructional techniques, know when each is appropriate and can implement them as needed. They are as aware of ineffectual or damaging practice as they are devoted to elegant practice.

They know how to engage groups of students to ensure a disciplined learning environment, and how to organize instruction to allow the schools' goals for students to be met. They are adept at setting norms for social interaction among students and between students and teachers. They understand how to motivate students to learn and how to maintain their interest even in the face of temporary failure.

Accomplished teachers can assess the progress of individual students as well as that of the class as a whole. They employ multiple methods for measuring student growth and understanding and can clearly explain student performance to parents.

4. **Teachers think systematically about their practice and learn from experience.**

Accomplished teachers are models of educated persons, exemplifying the virtues they seek to inspire in students — curiosity, tolerance, honesty, fairness, respect for diversity and appreciation of cultural differences — and the capacities that are prerequisites for intellectual growth: the ability to reason and take multiple perspectives to be creative and take risks, and to adopt an experimental and problem-solving orientation.

Accomplished teachers draw on their knowledge of human development, subject matter and instruction, and their understanding of their students to make principled judgments about sound practice. Their decisions are not only grounded in the literature, but also in their experience. They engage in lifelong learning which they seek to encourage in their students.

Striving to strengthen their teaching, accomplished teachers critically examine their practice, seek to expand their repertoire, deepen their knowledge, sharpen their judgment and adapt their teaching to new findings, ideas and theories.

5. **Teachers are members of learning communities.**

Accomplished teachers contribute to the effectiveness of the school by working collaboratively with other professionals on instructional policy, curriculum development and staff development. They can evaluate school progress and the allocation of school resources in light of their understanding of state and local educational objectives. They are knowledgeable about specialized school and community resources that can be engaged for their students' benefit, and are skilled at employing such resources as needed.

Accomplished teachers find ways to work collaboratively and creatively with parents, engaging them productively in the work of the school.

In 1987 the Board took on the messy and challenging task of defining quality teaching. It did not make judgments about best practices, weigh in on pedagogical debates, or rely on controversial standardized test scores. It identified the values, beliefs, and assumptions that underlie good teaching and expressed them as Five Core Propositions. In 1993 it began piloting a comprehensive performance assessment system that would identify accomplished teachers based on standards derived from the Core Propositions. And by 2002 there were over 23,000 teachers who had demonstrated that they were able to practice at the level of the accomplished teaching standards. These teachers had presented evidence—videotaped teaching events and student work samples—along with 40 to 60 pages of descriptive, analytic, and reflective writing; and they passed a rigorous test of their content knowledge to show that what they know and are able to do is aligned with the high and rigorous standards of the NBCTS. In the process, they were supported to put words to the complex challenges of their craft, to critically examine the choices they made to meet those challenges, and to thoughtfully consider the assumptions underlying their practice. They developed skills necessary for improvement.

The National Board movement, and its establishment of industry standards for quality teaching, has therefore initiated a cycle of capacity-building at the grassroots level. Teachers who pursue National Board Certification are not only better teachers for their own students but they are well-trained and well-positioned to facilitate the learning of their new and veteran teacher colleagues, to contribute to the conversation about student learning standards, to design curriculum and other resources, to change the culture of mediocrity so pervasive in teaching, to professionalize teaching by bringing teachers together under a common set of beliefs and external standards, to engage in practice-based research—all of which will help increase access to quality learning experiences for all children.

In the 10 years since its inception, National Board Teacher Certification has garnered ardent support from teachers, administrators, politicians, and policy makers. Hundreds of millions of public and private dollars have been allocated to support teachers who pursue this rigorous certification based on the collective hunch that it has a positive impact on teacher quality and student learning. Although passionate testimonials from teachers, administrators, and policy makers are easy to find, empirical studies have yet to be revealed that conclusively determine the impact of these teachers on student learning outcomes or on teaching culture (see Appendix A). These studies are admittedly difficult to produce; confounding factors such as student and teacher background, community characteristics, and school culture cannot be avoided when students are not randomly assigned to schools. Any attempts made to determine the value these teachers add to their students or their school communities must carefully consider how they will handle difficult questions: Aren't well-educated parents more likely to get their children into the classes of NBCTs? Mightn't NBCTs be dissimilar from one another in important ways that affect the study? Aren't NBCTs more likely to teach in schools with certain types of cultures? The limitations on studies of "teacher effects" are considerable.

In 1999, the first empirical study of National Board Teacher Certification was released. It did not attempt to prove any causal relationships, but showed that indeed National Board Certification is a "distinction that matters."[2] This study showed that on 11 out of 13 measures of teacher effectiveness, NBCTs outperformed their uncertified peers, and suggests that the National Board Certification process is able to identify accomplished teachers. But if we want to improve the quality of teaching and learning for all students, we have to be able to go beyond merely *identifying* accomplished teachers. We need to know how to *make* teachers into accomplished teachers.

Ninety-one percent of NBCTs who participated in a 2001 survey on the impact of National Board Certification self-reported that it has positively impacted their teaching practices and 93 percent report that they are better teachers.[3] Another survey of the same year found that 99.6 percent of NBCTs surveyed were involved in at least one leadership role (though on average they are involved in 10 leadership activities), and 89 percent of them "agreed that increased involvement in leadership activities makes them more effective as educators."[4] Although not scientifically rigorous enough to be conclusive on their own, preliminary studies such as these are encouraging; they suggest that National Board Certification has the potential to cause change in teachers, to improve the quality of teaching.

Over 50,000 teachers have pursued the National Board Certification process. These teachers approach the process for a myriad of reasons, with a diversity of levels of practice and with a variety of initial expectations. Some grow from the process. They feel recommitted to their students and the profession. They continue teaching with newfound confidence in their competence. They share successful teaching strategies. They seek out new leadership roles that will allow them to share their craft. Their increased facility to articulate the complicated processes of teaching and learning makes them key resources for policy makers, researchers, and the media. They create new schools, design innovative curricula, conduct action research, speak with the voice of expertise in education forums, collaborate with business partners, educate the media, advise legislators, and continue to pursue their own learning.

Others consider National Board Certification a feather in their cap, and return to working in the isolation of their own classroom with blinders firmly in place.

This book identifies the theory beneath why National Board Certification might improve the quality of teaching, and it makes strategic and practical recommendations about how it should be pursued based on that theory. It aims to maximize the professional development experience offered by National Board Certification. It is designed to ensure that teachers who take on National Board Certification because they want to become better teachers for their students, will be able to do so. And it is designed to help those who are positioned to support these teachers to know how they can help. Informed by a rich research base and the wisdom of 13 National Board Certified Teachers who have guided over 300 teachers through the process, this book was created to help improve the quality of teaching through National Board Certification.

Notes

1   NBPTS (1999). What Teachers Should Know and Be Able to Do. Southfield, MI, National Board for Professional Teaching Standards.

2   Bond, L., T. W. Smith, et al. (2000). The Certification System of the National Board for Professional Teaching Standards: A Construct and Consequential Validity Study. Greensboro, North Carolina, University of North Carolina at Greensboro.

3   NBPTS (2001). "I Am a Better Teacher." Southfield, MI, National Board for Professional Teaching Standards.

4   National Board for Professional Teaching Standards (2001). "The Impact of National Board Certification on Teachers: A Survey of National Board Certified Teachers and Assessors." Arlington, Virginia, National Board for Professional Teaching Standards: 6.

Part I

1. Improving the Practice of Teaching

The Power of Working in Groups

According to the U.S. Department of Education's examination of student performance on National Assessment of Education Progress (NAEP) scores from 1969 to 1999, student achievement in reading, math, and science has made only modest gains during the past 30 years.[1] Some argue further that this steady level is unacceptably low, especially in today's increasingly competitive world. An international comparison of student achievement in math and science showed that our twelfth-grade students were performing among the lowest of the developing and industrial countries participating in the study.[2] And a 1996 study showed that American schools are failing to provide the "new basic skills" that students need to be successful in the workplace and earn a middle-class wage.[3] These problems of student learning are exacerbated further by a significant and persistent achievement gap among students from low-income and minority families and the rest of the population.[4] By all these indicators, we see that the mediocre performance of students overall and the existence of an achievement gap by race and class point to a serious problem with student learning in American education.

A major campaign calling for higher-quality student learning was begun in 1983 in reaction to the publication of the book *Nation at Risk: The Imperative for Educational Reform.*[5] Since that time educational researchers, policy makers, and school site personnel have been searching in earnest for the elusive key to higher-quality student learning (see Figure 1.1). While they agree that student learning is the problem, they have different theories about the solution. Some argue that we need to *implement a new standards and accountability system* so that students, teachers, and schools will be clear about what all students should know and be able to do and can be held accountable for the levels of teaching and learning they achieve.[6] Another perspective suggests that in the face of an impending teacher shortage, we need to apply creative and thoughtful solutions to the problem of *attracting and retaining new teachers*.[7] Still others make the claim that the real problem lies in a *school and professional culture* that does not support high-quality teaching and learning.[8] Others are working to *focus educational research* more effectively on the pervasive problems of practice.[9] While it is true that in implementation these strategies can work together as part of a comprehensive plan, none of them can succeed without accomplished teachers. The key, therefore, to all of these education reform efforts is *improving the practice of teaching*.

> **Figure 1.1**
>
> **The Problem:**
> Mediocre performance of students overall and the existence of an achievement gap by race and class.
>
> **Proposed Solutions:**
>
> • Implement Standards and Accountability
>
> • Attract and Retain New Teachers
>
> • Influence School and Professional Culture
>
> • Build Stronger Connections Between Research and Practice
>
> • Improve the Practice of Teaching

Student learning is the direct result of a dynamic relationship between teachers, students, and curriculum[10] (see Figure 1.2). By *curriculum* I refer to both what and how teachers are teaching and students are learning. Curriculum may influence the choices a teacher makes in her teaching; that is, it may dictate how to approach the material and by what methods. It also may influence the choices the student makes in his learning, that is, whether to engage and how. The student may influence the curriculum choice, such that it must be developmentally appropriate and may even cater to student interests and needs. The student also may influence the teacher, in that his prior knowledge and his learning progress control the choices that the teacher makes about how to teach the material and in what order. The teacher, however, holds the power in this dynamic; she decides how much power the other two have.

To illustrate this point, let us consider the fact that today all 50 states have created standards that indicate what students need to know and be able to do, and many—but not all—districts provide resources that suggest methods by which their students might acquire this learning. Yet placing the students and the curriculum alone in a room together in most cases will not get results. The teacher is needed to use what she knows about

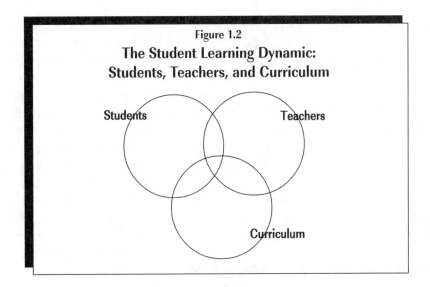

Figure 1.2
The Student Learning Dynamic:
Students, Teachers, and Curriculum

the curriculum and what she knows about the students to create meaning-ful learning experiences for her students. If she doesn't know the curriculum, doesn't know her students, or doesn't recognize her important role in connecting the two, learning is unlikely to take place.

Most life science curricula require that teachers teach observation skills. Students will need these skills as they engage in inquiry of various subjects within the field. Yet behind the closed door of her classroom, a teacher who does not have a solid mastery of this knowledge and skill herself may choose not to teach observation skills. She may choose other ways to cover the material, or may choose not to teach the material at all. When the principal comes in for evaluation, she will teach something she does know well. At the same time, a teacher who does have mastery of these skills makes important choices that will either help students to gain the factual knowledge and conceptual framework they need to develop true competence[11] or to remember enough of the facts to pass Friday's test. The teacher is in control of the content and depth of her students' learning.

Today we must recognize that our classrooms are full of students who represent a tremendous variety of diversity. They have different cultural backgrounds, different home experiences, different learning styles, different passions, and different core beliefs about the purpose of life and learning. They come to our classrooms with different perspectives and needs, yet the state hands us one set of standards to teach them all. In many schools the classroom door does not even have to be closed for a teacher to get away with teaching all of these different learners the same way. Yet, to return to our example of science instruction, an astute teacher of the blind would know enough to deviate from the dictated curriculum when it comes to teaching observation in life science. A teacher of English-language learners would recognize the life science lesson as a potent opportunity to introduce new vocabulary together with observation skills. A science teacher who knows that her students found a moldy lunch in the back of the room last period might take advantage of her students' interest and prior knowledge to build their observation skills from their preexisting experience. A teacher who has no knowledge of her students' diverse characteristics and background knowledge will be unable to make appropriate pedagogical choices to connect those students to the curriculum. The teacher is in control of the content and depth of her students' learning.

The critical point of entry, then, is the teacher. We need to make sure that teachers are making good teaching choices with respect to the curriculum and with respect to their students.

The contributions of other stakeholders should be acknowledged (see Figure 1.3). Parents and family members of the children we teach can be important partners in student learning. They can support their children so that these children can come into the learning dynamic ready to learn. Teachers have many strategies they may use to encourage parents to do this. At the same time, parents cannot truly be held accountable when they do not, and there is evidence that some children are able to succeed without this support.[12] Schools and other agencies do take advantage of this point of entry by making efforts to connect parents to educational opportunities, meal programs,

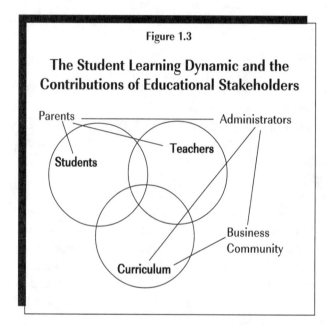

Figure 1.3

The Student Learning Dynamic and the Contributions of Educational Stakeholders

preschool programs, health care, and other services that assist parents in helping their children come to school ready to learn. While parent involvement is important, it is one step removed from the student-teacher-curriculum dynamic; parents do not exert the influence over student learning that teachers do.[13]

District and school-based administrators are another potential point of entry. They are responsible for creating an organizational structure that will support student learning. They are not only in the position of providing curricular resources and instructional leadership to enable teachers to work well but they also are in a position to foster community and parental involvement that will support students in their learning. From this point of view, we see that supporting these administrators to do their work effectively (through federal programs, professional associations, and interagency collaborations, for example) will, albeit indirectly, act on all three of the critical elements of the student learning dynamic. But administrators still do not exert the influence over student learning that teachers do.

The business community has a role here as well. Forward-thinking businesses have a vested interest in supporting education because they require a well-educated workforce and they know that a well-educated society is conducive to a healthy economy. While they cannot really be held accountable for not playing their part, the part that many of them do choose to play is critical. They agitate for policy to support high-quality learning through their business and political connections and they collaborate with schools by providing resources to help make it happen. They make an important contribution to the improvement of student learning but they, too, depend on teachers to make learning happen.

It is clear that teachers are the most efficacious point of entry in the activity of student learning. The National Commission for Teaching and America's Future (NCTAF) made this point clear in its 1996 statement *What Matters Most: Teaching for America's Future,*[14] in which it synthesized current research and declared, "What teachers know and can do is the most important influence on what students learn." The American Federation of Teachers (AFT) emphasized the same point in its 1995 manifesto: "The nation can adopt rigorous standards, set forth a visionary scenario, compile the best research about how students learn, change the nature of textbooks and assessment, promote teaching strategies that have been successful with a wide range of students, and change all the other elements involved in systemic reform. But unless the classroom teacher understands and is committed to the plan and knows how to make it happen, the dream will come to naught."[15] And when the National Alliance of Business (NAB) recently applied what it knows about costs and benefits, supply and demand, and smart business practices to the enterprise of education, it concluded: "The bottom line is clear—whatever else in the education structure we change—more challenging standards, different tests, new governance structures—our nation's efforts to lift student achievement will fail unless we have high quality teaching in every classroom."[16] Teachers cannot do it alone; they do depend on parents, administrators, business partners, and even students to work with them toward the goal of improved student learning, but teachers are in control of making learning happen. *Improving the quality of teaching holds the greatest promise for higher levels of student learning for all children.*

So we want to get teachers to teach better. This necessarily implies that what most teachers are currently doing is not adequate and that we want them to be doing something else. We are asking them to change—and we are hoping that the direction of the change will be positive.[17] Of the numerous teacher-quality initiatives that aim for teacher change, few clearly identify what they want teachers to change. Given the fact that change is so difficult and risky, and there is rarely an explicit reason to believe that the change will lead to improvement, it is no wonder that many teachers resist doing it.

Teachers are adults. Research tells us that adults will not change without recognition that there is a need, a cursory assessment that the change is logistically feasible, and a realistic vision of what the change will accomplish.[18] Are all teachers convinced that the problem of student learning is a serious one? Do they have a sense of efficacy about it? Do they think proposed changes will make enough difference to be worth the effort and risk? Teaching is extremely demanding work—intellectually, emotionally, and physically. When a teacher has found the magical combination of routines and resources that makes it all work, she is likely to stick with it unless there is a good reason to change, a reasonable prospect for improvement.

District and building-level administrators are in a position to give teachers a reason to change. They may make promises of support (such as a stipend or release from duties) or they may apply their influence in more indirect ways by making student achievement data publicly available or by sustaining a school culture to which teachers feel they have to conform. Teachers may have their own reasons to change their teaching as well. They may derive personal and professional satisfaction from learning new knowledge and skills that they feel will help to improve their teaching. In fact, research has shown that the most influential motivators for teachers are the intrinsic rewards of personal growth and being of service to their students.[19] But when none of these "good will" measures work to change the quality of teaching, there is always the option of bringing in more formal accountability.

Accountability systems involve measuring performance to standards of acceptable performance and applying rewards or sanctions accordingly. Administrators are in direct control of external accountability measures for teachers; they make regular evaluations of a teacher's performance using districtwide, union-approved teacher performance standards. Often presented in the form of a checklist of competencies, these standards may or may not be considered meaningful or fair to the parties involved, but job security usually rides on them. Given that these standards are the key to quality control in schools, it would be important to think critically about where they come from. Who makes them? What are they based on? Some districts look at teacher inputs (knowledge, skills, and dispositions), and others also consider student outcomes (student achievement scores). Who decides what to look at and where the bar is? Who is qualified to decide? In any accountability system, basic principles of behaviorism apply: Teacher change will depend on the strength of the rewards and sanctions. Teacher *improvement* will depend on the quality of the standards.

Administrators also have some control over internal accountability systems in schools. By offering recognition or opportunities for advancement to teachers who meet some kind of standard, teachers will have a reason to meet it. They will feel a sense of efficacy and accomplishment that will keep them accountable. Internal accountability measures are more palatable to teachers who recognize bonuses as manipulative and are more sustainable for teachers who feel coerced by job security threats. They are most effective when the recognition is genuine or opportunities for advancement are the result of actual good work. Again, clear, high-quality standards are required. Accountability may give teachers an incentive to change, but it does not address the most important problem: To what, exactly, are we asking teachers to change? We must have clearly articulated, high, and worthwhile goals because what we really want is not simply change, but improvement.

Initiatives that aim to improve the quality of teaching cannot rely on the "I'll know it when I see it" standard. They must be grounded in some theory about why the initiative is expected to change teaching practice in a positive direction. Appendix B provides a summary of some of the efforts that various stakeholders have made to improve the quality of teaching. Most of these efforts require a significant investment of time, money, and other resources on the part of both the public agencies and the individual people involved. Each has a rationale for why the initiative should be worth the investment, and each has some assumptions on which they depend.

Research grounds some of these efforts. Today there is some agreement about what characterizes "effective professional development," that is, professional development that improves the quality of teaching by causing changes in teaching practice that result in increased student learning. Effective professional development identified in this literature[20] enables teachers to use data to identify needs; it is job-embedded and ongoing; it brings teachers together in collaborative problem-solving around teaching and learning issues; it allows teachers to see the impact of their teaching; it provides multiple sources of information and theory on content, pedagogy, and child development; and it should be part of a comprehensive process. In fact, all of these characteristics can be evident in the process of National Board Certification—but only when pursued in groups.

- **It Enables Teachers to Use Data to Identify Needs**

  Many teachers today are supported in their schools to take time to look at student work collaboratively and to collect multiple perspectives on what the work has to say about individual student learning needs. It helps these teachers to know their students as learners, to develop plans for improvement, and to take collective responsibility for the students' success.[21] In fact, this same data source holds important clues about teacher learning needs. Looking at student work collaboratively can help teachers to know themselves as learners, to develop plans for their own improvement, and to take collective responsibility for a culture of improvement within the group. In the National Board Certification process, teachers spend several months collecting and reflecting on multiple forms of data—evidence of their teaching and their students' learning. They can use learning standards established by national professional associations, states, or the school community itself to help them identify student learning needs; these standards tell them what students should know and be able to do. What is the measuring stick for quality teaching? By establishing "high and worthwhile goals for what accomplished teachers should know and be able to do," the Board has provided an instrument for identifying teacher learning needs. When teachers work in groups to examine the data they collect and to measure it against these teaching standards, they increase their potential for professional growth. They can challenge one another's evidence, offer alternative interpretations of the data, and share strategies to address their own learning needs. Practical strategies are provided in Part II so that teachers can help one another use data to identify needs and collaborate for improved teaching practice.

- ### It Is Job-Embedded and Ongoing

  National Board Certification is an independent study course in the lab of one's own classroom. It is not an abstract exercise; it is grounded in teachers' actual experiences with their own students, at the current time, in their particular setting. Teachers typically spend between 4 and 7 months collecting evidence of the impact of their teaching on their students and comparing it to the NBTS Standards for Accomplished Teaching. Many teachers report that this process causes them to make changes in their teaching attitudes and behaviors.[22] But the literature on adult learning reminds us that it is very hard to *sustain* significant changes in behavior without significant changes in individuals' underlying meanings that may give rise to their behaviors.[23] When teachers use the evidence they collect to identify the assumptions that lie beneath their teaching choices and take time to help one another critically examine them with respect to the beliefs and assumptions which underlie good teaching (articulated in the Five Core Propositions), they are supported to make their tacit knowledge explicit, to make their invisible craft visible, and to recognize the control they exert on the quality of their teaching. By defending their teaching choices to one another, they hone their skills in the language of reflective practice. By putting their practice out to the group, they gain enough distance from it to recognize when intentional and thoughtful changes are needed. Part II includes activities that will support groups of teachers to use the National Board Certification experience to examine their assumptions and develop the reflective habits of mind that lead to an ongoing career of accomplished teaching.

- **It Brings Teachers Together in Collaborative Problem Solving around Teaching and Learning Issues**

  The process of National Board Certification focuses teachers' attention on the impact of their teaching on their students. Teachers who go through the process recognize how inefficient it is to be devising individual solutions to the collective problem of increasing student learning. There is a knowledge base shared by a professional community in education; while it has not been strategically coordinated, it is accessible through our professional associations, our journals, our workshops, and even our conversations with colleagues. (See Appendix D) The National Board Certification process is helping teachers to see the need to connect with it.[24] Teachers who pursue National Board Certification on their own forfeit this important opportunity to develop a community of practice around common conceptions of teaching and learning, to collaborate with others to solve the problems teachers share, and to benefit from the wisdom of their colleagues. Some of the activities in Part II help to bring teachers together around meaningful, practice-based exercises of collaborative problem solving. In this way, the certification process stands to have a much greater positive impact on those teachers' practice and on the teaching culture they share.

- **It Allows Teachers to See the Impact of Their Teaching**

  In the National Board Certification process teachers are guided through a very structured and systematic protocol for collecting evidence, analyzing and interpreting the data, and reflecting on the findings. It makes teachers into researchers where their own teaching and the resulting learning are the subject of their study. This process makes the impact of their teaching visible, and helps teachers gain a deeper understanding and sense of ownership of their own craft. Eleanor Duckworth has written extensively about the powerful experience of constructing one's own knowledge. She says of her students, be they children or adults:

  > First, in trying to make their thoughts clear for other people, students achieve greater clarity for themselves. Much of the learning is in the explaining. Second, the students themselves determine what it is they want to understand. It is not only the explanations that come from them, but also the questions. Third, people come to depend on themselves: They are judges of what they know and believe. They know why they believe it, what questions they still have about it, the degree of uncertainty about it, what they want to know next about it, how it relates to what other people think. Any other "explanation" they encounter must establish its place within what they know. Fourth, students recognize the powerful experience of having their ideas taken seriously, rather than simply screened for correspondence to what the teacher wanted....Fifth, students learn an enormous amount from

each other....Finally, learners come to recognize knowledge as a human construction, since they have constructed their own knowledge and they know that they have. What is written in a book is viewed as somebody else's creation, a creation produced just as they produced their own. Its origin is not of another order.[25]

Working in a group allows teachers to relate their observations to what others think, to take each other's ideas seriously, and to experience affirmation of their reconstructed knowledge. Part II includes activities that are designed to support teachers as they make visible and deconstruct the teaching practices they have picked up from colleagues, from their teacher preparation programs, even from the teachers from their own schooling—and reconstruct them to make them their own.

- **It Provides Multiple Sources of Information and Theory on Content, Pedagogy, and Child Development**

National Board Certification is aimed at accomplished teachers who know their subjects and know how to teach those subjects to their students. The Board does not provide the knowledge base required to achieve it. Most candidates, however, find that the process helps them to identify gaps in their practice or to recognize inconsistencies between their beliefs about teaching and their teaching choices. If National Board Certification is to *improve* the quality of teaching, not merely identify teachers who already meet the standards, teacher candidates will need access to multiple sources of information and theory on content, pedagogy, and child development that will help them to increase their knowledge and skills where necessary. Ideally one of these sources would be educational research; however, efforts to coordinate educational research in a way that makes it readily accessible to teachers have only recently begun.[26] Today's teachers who want to improve their knowledge and skills must be resourceful in identifying conferences, articles, Web sites, higher education courses, special programs, and colleagues that will give them the knowledge and skills they seek. (See Appendix D.) When candidates for National Board Certification are supported to work in groups, they can recommend resources and share their own expertise in ways that expand the knowledge and skills of others. Suggestions on how to do this are provided in Part II.

- ## It Should Be Part of a Comprehensive Process

National Board Certification is part of a comprehensive education reform effort that began in 1987. Today, with over 23,000 National Board Certified Teachers (NBCTs) in the United States, the National Board for Professional Teaching Standards (NBPTS) hopes to have one NBCT for each public school in the country by the year 2006. It is working to improve student learning by raising the standard of quality for teachers' practice. The National Board's Core Propositions articulate what all teachers—not just accomplished teachers—should know and be able to do. They also make it possible to bring an entire school staff or district together in a common conception of quality teaching and learning, and to create a culture that supports the improvement of teaching practice. Numerous states, districts, and schools have incorporated the National Board Certification process and/or the National Board's Standards into their education reform plans, with tremendous results (see Figure 1.4). Part II provides suggestions for how National Board candidates and National Board Certified Teachers can work together with their administrators to build comprehensive plans that will improve the quality of teaching practice throughout their school or district.

National Board Teacher Certification is considered by many to be an award, recognition, or even a prize. In fact, the National Board for Professional Teaching Standards itself has claimed that this advanced certification is "the highest honor the teaching profession has to bestow." At the same time, I submit that the extensive process of documentation and reflection that the National Board Certification process requires—when conducted together with colleagues—is more than an award; it is a powerful professional development experience. Many teachers do pursue it alone, whether due to practical considerations or personal preference. But working in groups is an important condition for making National Board Certification a powerful professional development experience. When teachers work in groups (two or more) to provide alternative interpretations of one another's evidence, to challenge one another's assumptions, to collaborate on problem solving, to support one another's experimentation and risk taking, to share knowledge and skills, and to nurture one another's learning, their teaching practice is more likely to change—in a positive direction. This book has been created to maximize the opportunities for professional growth afforded by National Board Certification. It aims to improve the practice of teaching.

Figure 1.4

Model Programs that Use the National Board's Standards and NBCTs to Improve the Quality of Teaching

Program	*Who*	*What*
Charlotte-Mecklen-burg School District in North Carolina (District with the second-largest number of NBCTs in the country) A program for professional develop-ment, candidate recruitment and support, public awareness, and public advocacy	Run by Charlotte-Mecklenburg Schools (three full-time teachers-in-residence), in collaboration with the University of North Carolina (UNCC) and Johnson C. Smith University (JCSU)	For **NBCT candidates:** • candidate fees paid • pay increases for those who achieve certification • career ladder opportunities For **district:** • NBCTs are taking on new roles • New capacity to tap for related reforms For **partners:** • Changing focus of teacher preparation at UNCC and JCSU • NBCTs serve as guest lecturers
Idaho Classrooms of Accomplished Teachers (ICAT) A program for professional develop-ment, support for new teachers	Idaho State University (ISU), Pocatello, ID	For **NBCTs:** • A new differentiated role For **preservice teachers:** • ISU uses videotapes of accomplished teaching (Quality Visions) to demonstrate the standards of quality teaching. For **new teachers:** • Idaho districts use videotapes to guide new teachers through structured analyses of the performances • New teachers are paired with mentors For **all teachers:** • Teachers are being trained to facilitate professional development using the tapes • At least one district in ID has made the tapes the main focus of professional development for the district
Santa Monica Malibu Schools A program for Candidate support, and professional development	Santa Monica Malibu Schools superintendent and school board, Santa Monica Malibu Classroom Teachers Association leadership, local business community representa-tives, and University of California at Los Angeles	For **NBCT candidates:** • Support aimed at 100% success rate • Salary increase upon certification • Recognition • Career ladder opportunities For **district:** • Professional development is coordinated through a new "Professional Development and Leadership Center" grounded in National Board standards • Revised teacher evaluation system (and eventually the administrator evaluation system)

cont.

| RHODE Program (Recognition and Honoring of Outstanding Demonstrated Excellence), Coventry, RI

A program to improve the quality of teaching through professional development and performance pay | Coventry Leadership (superintendent, assistant superintendent, and professional development director), Coventry Teachers' Alliance (union) leadership, Educational Issues Department of the American Federation of Teachers | For **NBCT candidates:**
• Candidate support
• Pay increases upon certification
• Career ladder opportunities
For **all teachers:**
• A new high standard of quality teaching to which all teachers can aspire.
• A new teacher evaluation system aligned to that vision.
• Performance pay based on the teacher evaluation system.
• A new resource to help them mprove: a "Professional Development and Leadership Center" |

Notes

1. National Center for Education Statistics, *NCES Digest of Education Statistics* (2000 [cited 2002]); available from nces.ed.gov/pubs2001/digest.

2. OERI, *TIMSS: More About the Project* (U.S. Department of Education, 2002 [cited 2002]); available from http://nces.ed.gov/timss/timss95/index.asp.

3. Richard J. Murnane and Frank Levy, *Teaching the New Basic Skills: Principles for Educating Children to Thrive in a Changing Economy* (New York: The Free Press, 1996).

4. C. Jencks, Phillips, M., "The Black-White Test Score Gap: An Introduction," in *The Black-White Test Score Gap*, ed. C. Jencks, Phillips, M. (Washington, D.C.: Brookings Institution Press, 1991); National Center for Education Statistics, *NCES Digest of Education Statistics* (cited).

5. National Commission on Excellence in Education, "A Nation at Risk: The Imperative for Educational Reform," (Washington, D.C.: 1983).

6. Diane Ravitch, "National Standards in American Education: A Citizen's Guide," (Washington, D.C.: Brookings Institution, 1995); Mark S. Tucker and Judy B. Codding, "Setting High Standards for Everyone," in *Standards for Our Schools: How to Set Them, Measure Them, and Reach Them* (San Francisco: Jossey-Bass, 1988).

7. Thomas B. Fordham Foundation, "The Teachers We Need and How to Get More of Them: A Manifesto," in *Better Teachers, Better Schools*, ed. Jr. M. Kanstoroom & C. Finn (Washington, D.C.: Thomas B. Fordham Foundation, 1999); Heather G. Peske et al., "The Next Generation of Teachers: Changing Conceptions of a Career in Teaching," *Phi Delta Kappa*, December 2001.

8. Robert Evans, "The Culture of Resistance," in *The Jossey-Bass Reader on School Reform* (San Francisco: Jossey-Bass, 2001); J. Saphier, King, M., "Good Seeds Grow in Strong Cultures," *Educational Leadership* 1985.

9. National Research Council, "A Strategic Education Research Partnership to Bridge Research and Practice," (Washington, D.C.: The National Academies Press, 2002).

10. David Hawkins, "I, Thou and It," in *The Informed Vision: Essays on Learning and Human Nature*, ed. David Hawkins (New York: Agathon Books, 1974). Representation of Hawkins' theory as Venn diagram comes from Richard Elmore.

11. John D. Bransford, Ann L. Brown, and Rodney R. Cocking, eds., *How People Learn: Brain, Mind, Experience and School*, Expanded Edition ed. (Washington, D.C.: National Academy Press, 2000).

12. James H. McMillan and Daisy F. Reed, "At-Risk Students and Resiliency: Factors Contributing to Academic Success," *The Clearing House* 67 (1994).

13. The Coleman report (Coleman, 1966) suggested in 1966 that the effects of schooling could never fully overcome the effects of the home, or socioeconomic status. Sanders' more recent research (Sanders & Rivers, 1996) challenges this traditional notion and establishes teacher effectiveness as the most important influence on student achievement.

14. Linda Darling-Hammond, "What Matters Most: Teaching for America's Future," (New York: National Commission on Teaching and America's Future, 1996).

15. American Federation of Teachers, "Principles for Professional Development," (Washington, D.C.: American Federation of Teachers, 1995).

16. National Alliance of Business, "Investing in Teaching," (Washington, DC: National Alliance of Business, 2001).

17. For my keen attention to the direction of change in education reforms efforts, credit is due to Richard Elmore.

18. Michael Fullan, *The New Meaning of Education Reform* (New York: Teachers' College Press, 2001); Phillip C. Schlechty, *Schools for the 21st Century: Leadership Imperatives for Educational Reform* (San Francisco: Jossey-Bass Publishers, 1990).

19. Paul Bredeson, Marvin Firth, and Katherine Kasten, "Organizational Incentives and Secondary School Teaching," *Journal of Research and Development in Education* 16, no. 4 (1983); Dan C. Lortie, *Schoolteacher* (Chicago: The University of Chicago Press, 1975).

20. Michael Garet et al., "What Makes Professional Development Effective? Results from a National Sample of Teachers," *American Educational Research Journal* 38, no. 4 (2001); W. Hawley, & L.Valli, "The Essentials of Professional Development: A New Consensus," in *Teaching as the Learning Profession: Handbook of Policy and Practice*, ed. G. Sykes & L. Darling-Hammond (San Francisco: Jossey-Bass, 1999); Michael Huberman, "Networks That Alter Teaching: Conceptualizations, Exchanges, and Experiments," *Teachers and Teaching: Theory and Practice* 1, no.2 (1995); Anne C. Lewis, "A New Consensus Emerges on the Characteristics of Good Professional Development," *Harvard Education Letter*, (May/ June 1997); Dennis Sparks and Steven Hirsh, "A New Vision for Staff Development," (National Staff Development Council (NSDC) and Association for Supervision and Curriculum Development (ASCD), 1997).

21. Tina Blythe, David Allen, and Barbara S. Powell, *Looking Together at Students' Work: A Companion Guide to Assessing Student Learning* (New York: Teachers' College Press, 1999); Kathleen Cushman, "Looking Collaboratively at Student Work: An Essential Toolkit," *Horace*, (November 1996).

22. National Board for Professional Teaching Standards, "I Am a Better Teacher," (Southfield, MI: National Board for Professional Teaching Standards, 2001).

23. Robert Kegan and Lisa Laskow Lahey, *How the Way We Talk Can Change the Way We Work* (San Francisco: Jossey-Bass, 2001).

24. In fact, in a 2001 NBPTS survey, 74% of NBCTs reported that achieving National Board Certification affected their professional roles. The new roles they took on

ranged from serving on committees, to mentoring NBCT candidates, to working with colleagues.

25. Eleanor Duckworth, *"the Having of Wonderful Ideas" and Other Essays on Teaching and Learning* (New York: Teachers College Press, 1987). p. 131.

26. OERI has supported the development of AskEric (www.AskEric.com), a Web-based resource that enables teachers to identify the research they need to inform their teaching. Initially developed 10 years ago, this service has a new, user-friendly interface.

2. Improving the Culture of Teaching

The Potential of NBCTs

ABCDeFG hiL KLMNO PQrstuvWx

When teachers use the National Board Certification experience to improve the quality of their teaching practice, there are substantial benefits for the teachers and their students. Students can expect higher levels of learning as a result of their teachers' heightened ability to create powerful, effective, and appropriate learning opportunities. Teachers can become beneficiaries of both intrinsic and extrinsic benefits. They gain a sense of confidence in their teaching competence as well as an increased sense of satisfaction in their work. They also may receive recognition, offers for new leadership roles, or financial compensation as a result of their successful completion of National Board Certification. With these benefits in mind, some teachers happily pay over $2000 out of their own pockets to pursue it.

But public and private foundation monies—to the tune of hundreds of millions of dollars—are being allocated with remarkable enthusiasm to support teachers who pursue National Board Certification. This funding has significantly influenced the growth of National Board Certification, as it subsidizes assessment fees, candidate support groups, salary bonuses for teachers who successfully achieve certification, and/or outreach efforts. This being the case, it is important to consider what the public actually receives in return for this investment, and how the benefits of those same dollars might be maximized.

The question of how to increase student learning is a daunting national conundrum which teachers, administrators, researchers, and policy makers are working on from every angle. National Board Teacher Certification may improve learning for the individual students in certified teachers' classrooms, but the National Board Certification process is neither appropriate nor feasible for all teachers. It is available only to teachers who have at least 3 years of licensed teaching experience, and it is available only to the 95 percent of teachers who are teaching in the areas for which assessments have been developed. It has an extensive written component that poses a significant challenge to many teachers, and it requires a significant amount of time and mental energy that the candidate must be prepared to commit. Above all, it is voluntary. Since not all teachers can or want to pursue National Board Certification, an important question then presents itself: Under what conditions might National Board Certification make an impact on teaching and learning beyond the classroom of the National Board Certified Teacher?

Current efforts to improve student learning at a systemic level fall into five main categories: imposing standards and accountability, attracting and retaining new teachers, improving school and professional culture, connecting research and practice, and improving the practice of teaching. (See Figure 2.1). Each of these efforts makes assumptions about capacity that are not necessarily grounded in the reality of the majority of today's schools. By establishing an industry standard for what teachers should know and be able to do, and by supporting the growth of a corps of teachers who have a demonstrated capacity to meet those standards, the National Board's work stands to advance these related education reforms by providing the capacity necessary for their success.

Figure 2.1

Identifying quality teaching through National Board's Certification helps to create the conditions necessary for other reforms to succeed:

- Imposing standards and accountability

- Attracting and retaining new teachers

- Improving school and professional culture

- Connecting research and practice

- Improving the practice of teaching

Teachers who are National Board Certified have demonstrated that they are able to practice at the level of the standards. While further research is needed to learn more about the specific knowledge and skills that are honed in teachers through the National Board Certification process, we do know that these teachers report significant changes in their attitudes and behaviors. They are more articulate about their practice, they know how to use data to make informed teaching choices, and they are better teachers for their students. They have a lot of capacity that can be tapped in the service of other reforms. When NBCTs are given new and differentiated roles, they are able to make an impact on the culture of teaching that will reach far beyond their own classrooms.

Standards and Accountability

In response to the rising accountability movement initiated by the publication of *Nation at Risk*[1] and with the endorsement of the National Governors' Council in 1989, national professional organizations began creating curriculum standards that articulate what students should know and be able to do for every subject area and developmental level.[2] States and some districts have used these documents together with input from educational stakeholders to create their own standards. It may be faulty to assume that all educational stakeholders have the capacity to weigh in on the drafting of rigorous and comprehensive standards. NBCTs need to be in on the conversation.

The task of assessing students' knowledge and skill based on these comprehensive standards has some logistical and financial implications that are necessarily limiting. It is not practical to observe authentic performances by every single student that demonstrate every single standard. On the other hand, teachers need comprehensive assessment feedback that can inform their instruction. These considerations have led most states and districts to administer assessments that can be standardized and scored quickly, a compromise that penalizes teachers who take the time to teach all of the standards (oral language, the arts, social curriculum, and so on) not just those that are tested. Most states use multiple-choice tests; others augment these tests with open response questions. A few states such as Vermont and Kentucky and many districts in other states have experimented with assessing authentic performances through portfolios in an effort to obtain a more holistic and accurate assessment of children. All assessments are necessarily limited; they must make trade-offs between what they want to be able to say about students or programs and practical considerations of money and logistics.

With standards and assessment in place, it is important to consider who will be held accountable for assessment results, how, and by whom. If teachers are held accountable, they will be sure to teach the content in the standards. If students are held accountable, they will be more likely to be motivated to learn. If districts are held accountable, they will work hard to ensure that teachers and students have what they need to make learning happen... or so the theory goes. States and districts have used a variety of sanctions and rewards for teachers (job security or salary bonuses), students (diplomas withheld or recognition), and districts (public sanctions or recognition that have an impact on reputation and real estate). In sum, the improvement theory implicit in the standards and accountability strategy is that when high and worthwhile standards are set for what students need to know and be able to do and stakeholders are held accountable for making sure students have opportunities to learn them, student learning will improve.

But the key to the success of this theory is that teachers and districts whose students fail to meet the standards *know how* to improve. It is not enough to merely know what needs improving. Teachers need to know how to teach the standards more effectively. They need to know how to use data to inform instruction; they need to know how to develop a keen knowledge of their students; and they need to know how to teach their content to those students.

National Board Certified Teachers are well trained to be instructional leaders. Their extensive experience with collecting and critically examining a variety of evidence, of measuring the evidence against standards for accomplished teaching, and of using reflection to make midcourse changes in their teaching gives them the experience to say that they know what good teaching looks like and the rhetorical skills to explain why it is good. Their experience in improving their own practice can help them to support the improvement of others. The National Board Certification process has helped them to develop the habits of mind that all teachers need to systematically analyze and reflect on their teaching practice. They are well versed in the NBPTs Core Propositions, the industry standard for quality teaching. And they are well positioned to work with their colleagues in improving their practice through teacher preparation programs, peer coaching, demonstration lessons, and mentoring. Their impact on teaching and learning can go far beyond their own classrooms if they are offered these new roles.

Attracting and Retaining Teachers

Stakeholders who recognize the important role teachers play in student learning also recognize that student learning is likely to improve if there is a system regulating who gets to teach. Licensing requirements vary from state to state to include everything from a simple background check to daylong content knowledge examinations. Many states base their licensing requirements on draft standards created by the Interstate New Teacher Assessment and Support Consortium (INTASC). Some teacher education programs go further to meet the more stringent requirements of the National Council for Accreditation of Teacher Education (NCATE). In either case, the standards set by these professional organizations aim to ensure that new teachers will be prepared with basic competencies and a clear idea of the task ahead of them.[3] Yet not all teacher preparation programs follow these standards.

At the same time, current trends of retirement and attrition in the teaching force are working together to threaten a teacher shortage.[4] Most states have begun to respond by offering waivers and alternative routes to licensure that bypass some of these quality controls in order to ensure that each classroom has at least someone at the front of it. By removing barriers to entry and in some cases providing incentives to new teachers, strategists have succeeded in attracting more people to teaching, but they risk jeopardizing quality.

This raises three serious issues that must be confronted. First, these new teachers may be well-meaning, caring, and competent in their content, but if they do not know how to effectively teach that content to their students, they in fact are doing a great disservice to their students as they exacerbate the problem of the achievement gap. Research tells us of the importance of teacher effectiveness. While we know that teachers are the most important influence on student learning, pioneering work conducted in 1996 illustrated the additive and cumulative effects of effective and ineffective teachers. It found, for example, that 1 year with an ineffective teacher has an impact on that student's achievement that can be seen 2 years later.[5] Where do most unlicensed, ineffective, and unprepared teachers end up? In the schools with the greatest need for quality teachers. It is therefore unacceptable to create a plan to attract and retain teachers without serious consideration of how those teachers will learn to be effective teachers...quickly. The National Board's Core Propositions can help newcomers to the profession from any route to identify what it is they need to work on to become effective teachers, and National Board Certified Teachers in the district are well placed to serve as mentors as these newcomers develop their craft. They are brimming with the capacity to take on this important role.

Second, by disregarding the importance of pedagogical knowledge, some alternative certification programs misrepresent teaching as so easy that anyone who has gone to school can do it. This does a disservice to the profession for two reasons. It causes many to see teaching as something they will do for a little while or as a break between "real jobs." It helps to bury for good the notion of a career teacher. Initial findings from Harvard University's Project on the Next Generation of Teachers suggest that "rather than regarding teaching as a calling and a lifelong commitment, many new teachers—both those who completed traditional teacher preparation programs and those who did not—approach teaching tentatively or conditionally."[5] These teachers feel patronized by their entrepreneurial peers who have to explain what they do; teaching somehow seems to need no explanation. Further, representing teaching as easy may help more people to decide to teach, but it does little to curb the low retention rate. Teachers who enter teaching thinking it will be easy are less likely to ask for and accept help. Research shows that nearly 30 percent of new teachers leave teaching before their third year and nearly 40 percent leave teaching before their fifth anniversary.[7] While it is true that some of these short-term teachers only had 1 to 3 years of teaching in their plan, many others hoped to stay longer but found the job more difficult than they expected and had little to no support. Using the Core Propositions as a guide for what all teachers should know and be able to do, NBCTs can guide these teachers to understand the extent of the career they have committed to, and support them in developing a plan to improve their teaching practice.

Lastly, when people choose to teach, they should plan to be good

teachers. There should be a plan in place that will induct these fresh re-
cruits to the standards of the profession. The notion that the teaching
profession has certain core competencies is overlooked by many. The
National Board's Five Core Propositions provide for those considering a
"spin" in the classroom a clear definition of the beliefs and values that bind
the profession they plan to enter. It explains with clarity the nature of the
task. It tells them what all teachers should know and be able to do. All
prospective teachers should enter the profession with these benchmarks in
mind and with strategies in place for how they plan to reach them. NBCTs
can be on hand to help them work toward these goals. Further, the existence of National Board Teacher Certification provides a career trajectory
for teachers; it turns teaching into a profession with opportunities for advancement, a profession held together by a common conception of quality
teaching, a profession people will want to join and in which they will be
proud to remain.

The national problem of attracting and retaining quality teachers is not
going to go away. NBCTs have the capacity to be an important part of the
solution.

School and Professional Culture

The qualities of teaching and learning are influenced by the professional culture in which they are embedded. School cultures that value
collegiality, share responsibility, and hold high professional goals are asso-
ciated with higher student achievement.[8] In these schools, teachers support one another to improve the quality of their teaching. They view a
healthy culture as an incentive to stay in the profession; and in the school
that nurtures it, teacher mobility rates are lower.[9]

Culture, however, is not an easy force to influence. It consists of the
fundamental assumptions and beliefs that are shared by members of a
group, operating unconsciously to determine the way things are done.[10]
When attention is not paid to nurturing shared assumptions of high expectations, the shared assumptions fall to the lowest common denominator.
Any energetic new teacher or visionary veteran who joins such a culture
will find it hard to resist becoming quickly acclimated to the stagnant culture. Schools become organized around dysfunctional norms; and the routines, policies, even architectural features, build up to support "the way
things have always been done." Reforms that aim to improve school culture, therefore, take on a gargantuan twofold task. They must bring a teaching
force—whose members espouse diverse beliefs, backgrounds, and experiences and have some inevitable degree of turnover—to develop a common set of beliefs and assumptions about teaching and learning. Then,
they must bring the staff to trust one another enough to take the risks and
exert the effort needed to go up against the way the school has organized
itself and change the structures supporting the ways things have always

been done. Teachers will not easily give up their fundamental beliefs and assumptions about teaching—and the autonomy they enjoy—just because an administrator says that it's time to build a new culture. They will take into consideration, among other things, the feasibility or complexity of the task, and the likelihood that the change will result in actual improvement.[11]

The task truly is complex. It seems infeasible for a school's staff to spend the time it would take to develop and agree upon standards for what its teachers should know and be able to do in order to produce high levels of learning. One might also question whether they have the capacity to do so, since the members may not be well informed about current issues in education and advancements in relevant educational research. Even if they could, administrators would then have to meet the challenges of maintaining a high level of agreement on those standards despite inevitable staff turnover and helping the staff translate their new beliefs and assumptions into new ways of doing things.

The work of the National Board for Professional Teaching Standards (NBPTS) has removed some of the complexity of this important task. It has brought together a diverse group of education professionals—from classroom practitioners to educational researchers to teacher trainers; from public, private, and parochial schools; from every region of the country; and from every race, political persuasion, and gender—to determine together what every teacher should know and be able to do. In doing so, it has established an industry standard that is grounded in the expertise of hundreds of teachers and thousands of years of teaching experience. This standard, also referred to as the Five Core Propositions, is worth examining critically (see Introduction, Figure 0.2). Teachers will find that it can initiate powerful conversations about quality teaching. As a national standard, it carries the authority to support newcomer buy-in, and as the basis of National Board Certification, it offers a structure to help develop the capacity needed to model the standards and to incorporate them into all levels of practice. National Board Certified Teachers are well-positioned and well-trained to help their new and veteran colleagues examine their assumptions, and to recreate teacher evaluation and compensation structures that are aligned to the standards.

It is important here to recall the distinction between change and improvement. Our goal is not to merely change school culture, but to improve it. Our goal is not merely to unite teachers' conceptions of teaching, but to have them share a common conception of quality teaching that will result in higher levels of student learning. Everyone has his or her own story about a favorite teacher, an "effective" teacher who challenged him or her to reach new heights. And everyone's story is different. These stories give us grounded ideas about what good teaching is, and cast doubt on the idea that there might be one "right" way to teach. At the same time, if the teachers in this learning community are to do more than change—to improve—then there needs to be a clear, rigorous, and comprehensive standard that articulates what "quality teaching" is. This standard does not imply that fail-proof "best practices" exist that can be identified and replicated throughout classrooms everywhere. Rather it implies that there are beliefs, values, and assumptions or Core Propositions, which can guide teachers in making good choices about which practices will most effectively increase a student's opportunity to learn, given his or her individual needs and the unique characteristics of the context. These beliefs, values, and assumptions are universal. They transcend pedagogical styles, partisan lines, and personalities. Once teachers engage with them and see them in their own practice, they come together with a unity of purpose, and the beliefs and assumptions they share determine a new higher denominator. This is the case in Charlotte-Mecklenburg, North Carolina, in the Los Angeles Unified District, and in Coventry, Rhode Island, where a critical mass of NBCTs has been achieved. This is also the case with isolated NBCTs who tend to either seek out that professional solidarity or create it themselves. National Board Certified Teachers travel to national conferences, subscribe to professional journals, and are active participants in NBCT listservs, but too many of them ignore their own school sites. If districts want to harness the capacity of NBCTs locally, they need to recognize the potential of these accomplished teachers and invite them to take on new roles that will capitalize on their expertise.

Isolation is a common and chronic characteristic of school culture.[12] Many teachers do not discuss the work of their classrooms with their colleagues beyond anecdotal storytelling, and they follow an unspoken closed-door policy. Teaching cultures with a strong status quo invite comparison and competition, yet innovation is often viewed with disdain or jealousy—a threat to the sense of community. If teachers in a school community could agree on a common conception of quality teaching, a significant barrier to sharing practice could be overcome. Instead of subjecting their practice to competitive judgment, teachers could measure their practice up to a high and worthwhile external and objective standard. In this way teachers may begin to see one another as resources to support professional growth. They may develop common ground rules for peer and administrator observations, and through discussion they may develop a common rhetoric to talk about, analyze, and learn from one another's teaching. Teachers would see that their work is a part of something larger than their own classroom, larger than their school, and is in fact part of a profession guided by common national standards.

Another related and problematic characteristic of teaching culture is manifest in teachers who believe they know it all. Many of us grew up in environments where the students had all the questions and the teachers had all the answers. We memorized facts and reported them back on weekly tests. In today's diverse, technological, and rapidly changing society, memorizing facts is not nearly as important as using one's mind well. Teachers must be facilitators of learning. They must be prepared to learn from students, from colleagues, from the ever-growing body of educational research and from their own practice. They must help students to gain knowledge, while also giving students a sense of how knowledge is being constructed, deconstructed, and reconstructed every day. NBCTs have had the humbling yet empowering experience of having their expertise deconstructed, and they have proved through their portfolios that they are members of learning communities. They model for their students and colleagues the benefits of life-long learning. When teachers are united in their belief that good teachers are good learners, they support one another to ask questions, take risks, and make changes in the way they do things—they support a healthy teaching culture.

National Board Certified Teachers, teachers who have shown that they can practice at the level of the standards for accomplished teaching, can play a critical role in the evolution of teaching culture. When districts support teachers to pursue National Board Certification, they are building capacity; they are training instructional leaders who can lead from the classroom, and they are building the critical mass it takes to raise the bar on teaching culture.

Connecting Research and Practice

When research advancements are announced in the field of medicine, doctors everywhere begin using the new knowledge within weeks to conduct their work more effectively. Educational research does not have a similar tradition of connecting with the world of educational practice. A variety of reasons have been given to explain this disconnect. There are logistical issues involved in identifying lab sites where sustained research is possible and in making the research practically and intellectually accessible. There can be political issues involved in coordinating the replication of research and the elaboration of that research into products that will reach the classroom. There are practical issues as well: Researchers are not rewarded for interactions with practitioners; it is not part of the culture of higher education. As a result of these issues, researchers pay too little attention to the most important problems of practice and to related topics of teacher learning and organizational learning.[13] Given that research plays such an important guiding role in the practice of so many other professions, it is interesting to consider how the National Board's work might contribute toward efforts to bring educational research and practice together. There are three main ways: It may help teachers develop rhetorical skills that will help bridge the languages of research and practice, it may pique teachers' interest in participating in research, and it may make workable partnerships easier to identify.

Whether groups of teachers are working on National Board Certification or are merely engaging in conversations about the Core Propositions, they are developing a shared language with which to describe the very complicated and often unconscious processes of teaching and learning. Teachers know that certain practices feel right, they see that they work, but they often do not have a need to put this tacit knowledge into words that clearly communicate to others what they are doing and why. In fact, National Board Candidates typically get about 6 to 8 months of regular oral and written exercise in talking about their practice. The conversations among teachers generated by National Board work, whether they are critically examining a videotaped teaching event or debating the characteristics of quality teaching at a staff meeting, push teachers to develop their rhetorical skills in ways that make them valuable resources for researchers, as well as others. When teachers have the words to discuss their teaching, they increase their power to improve it when working with researchers and others.

The National Board Certification process also helps to close the cultural gap between teachers and researchers. National Board Candidates begin to think of themselves as researchers, working in the lab of their own classrooms to understand the impact of their own teaching on their students' learning. They collect data, analyze and interpret it, then reflect on the evidence to produce findings or draw conclusions that inform next steps. They see how a focused inquiry process can have an impact on student learning and on their satisfaction with their professional lives. It is a process these teachers find illuminating and invigorating and which researchers find familiar. Many NBCTs are attracted to pursue more formal research projects after this experience, collaborating with colleagues to conduct their own action research or seeking out collaborations with researchers.

While teachers may seek out collaborations with researchers, the arrangement more commonly works the other way around. Researchers typically have a variety of hit-or-miss strategies they use to find cooperating practitioners who are able to weigh in with the wisdom of practice in their projects. By pursuing National Board Certified Teachers as research partners, researchers may find that they can make quicker work of identifying workable and mutually beneficial partnerships.

As partnerships develop and teachers and researchers begin to develop a rapport around classroom practice, teachers will be better able to clearly communicate to researchers the areas of educational research that are most needed from their classroom perspective. And researchers will be better able to communicate their findings to teachers in ways that will be well received by teachers. This partnership has advantages for both parties, but it benefits students the most: They will be the beneficiaries of quality research that is aimed at improving student learning.

Improving the Practice of Teaching

Districts, states, and even the federal government have tried to make an impact on student learning from a systemic level by improving the practice of teaching through professional development. They pour millions of dollars into a variety of activities each year. It is important to consider the impact of the professional activities these resources support.

Some aim to strengthen teacher knowledge of content or child development through coursework; others introduce teachers to new pedagogical strategies through workshops, and still others build capacity through trained coaches. There are on-site whole staff retreats, weeklong summer institutes, and release-day workshops. Teachers participate in these activities as required by licensing regulations, and their own academic interests or their own perception of their professional growth needs often guide their choices. A workshop here, a course there, some relevant, some less so, but licensing credit given nonetheless…

What if these activity choices were guided by a plan, a plan with an unwavering focus on improving student learning? A plan that was shared by teachers in a school, by teachers in a state, by the profession as a whole? The National Board's Core Propositions for what every teacher should know and be able to do give focus to systemic coordination of professional development. Teacher evaluation, peer observation, and self-reflection activities should be guided by these Propositions in order to help teachers recognize the areas of their practice that need growth. Workshops, courses, and summer institutes should be provided based on these Propositions to give teachers the knowledge and skills they need to meet the Standards. And when teachers feel as though their practice meets the Standards for Accomplished Teachers, they should be supported to work in groups to pursue National Board Certification. Once certified, districts need to capitalize on their expertise and continue to support their learning. They need to present NBCTs with new roles that rechannel their expertise into a cycle of capacity-building: standards committee members, trainers and mentors for new teachers, instructional leaders, research partners, professional development coaches, and so on. This pattern describes a career ladder for teachers that will support their ongoing personal and professional growth, their ability to make an impact on teaching culture, and their ability to increase learning for all students.

The National Board for Professional Teaching Standards does not guarantee that National Board Certified Teachers always do or always will practice at the level of the Standards. It stands to reason that certain professional conditions would support some teachers to sustain the benefits of the experience more than others. My claim is that when NBCTs become involved in new roles that capitalize on their expertise, they not only will be more likely to maintain the high standards of accomplished teaching but they will improve the quality of teaching culture. Part II includes specific strategies for sharing the capacity of NBCTs.

Inadequate and unequal student learning is a fundamental problem in America today. What kind of profession allows its members to devise individual solutions to a collective problem? If we want to have quality at scale, we have to have standards at scale. In establishing national standards to guide the improvement of the culture of teaching, members of the teaching profession have come together with unity of purpose to devise a solution.

Notes

1.   National Commission on Excellence in Education, "A Nation at Risk: The Imperative for Educational Reform," (Washington, D.C.: 1983).

2.   The National Council of Teachers of Mathematics (NCTM), the National Council for Teachers of English (NCTE), the National Research Council (NRC) which coordinated development of science standards, etc.

3.   Both of these organizations have aligned their standards to those of NBPTS.

4.   W. J. Hussar, *Predicting the Need for Newly Hired Teachers in the United States to 2008-9* (Washington, D.C.: National Center for Education Statistics, 1999).

5.   William L. Sanders and June C. Rivers, "Cumulative and Residual Effects of Teachers on Future Student Academic Achievement," (Knoxville, TN: University of Tennessee Value-Added Research and Assessment Center, 1996).

6.   Heather G. Peske et al., "The Next Generation of Teachers: Changing Conceptions of a Career in Teaching," *Phi Delta Kappa*, (December 2001).

7.   Richard M. Ingersoll, "A Different Approach to Solving the Teacher Shortage Problem," *Teaching Quality: Policy Briefs*, no. 3 (2001).

8.   Judith Warren Little, "Norms of Collegiality and Experimentation: Workplace Conditions of School Success," *American Educational Research Journal* 19, no. 3 (1982), Susan Rosenholtz, Otto Bassler, and Kathy Hoover-Dempsey, "Organizational Conditions of Teacher Learning," *Teaching and Teacher Education* 2, no. 2 (1986).

9.   Edgar H. Schein, *Organizational Culture and Leadership, Jossey-Bass Management Series* (San Francisco: Jossey-Bass, 1992).

10. Michael Fullan, *The New Meaning of Education Reform* (New York: Teachers' College Press, 2001).

11. Judith Warren Little, "The Persistence of Privacy: Autonomy and Initiative in Teachers' Professional Relations," *Teachers College Record* 91, no. 4 (1990).

12. National Research Council, "A Strategic Education Research Partnership to Bridge Research and Practice," (Washington, D.C.: The National Academies Press, 2002).

Part II

---

3. Improving the Practice of Teaching

A Toolkit for Candidate Groups

Teachers who want to improve the quality of teaching through National Board Certification— and those who support them— should understand that National Board Certification is at once a rigorous assessment system and a challenging professional development exercise.

National Board Certification is an assessment. Candidates follow a strictly defined protocol as they prepare a selection of evidence to provide to assessors *clear, consistent, and convincing* evidence that they are able to practice at the level of the Standards for Accomplished Teaching. Practitioners from the same certificate area who are trained to examine the evidence and evaluate it based on scoring rubrics, assess the work and provide a score.

National Board Certification is a professional development exercise. Candidates follow a strictly defined protocol that guides them in collecting data on their students' learning, in documenting their teaching choices, in analyzing the teaching and learning that have occurred, and in making realizations about how to improve the effectiveness of their teaching. It helps them to clearly see the impact of their teaching on their students and to understand what underlies effective teaching so that they can ensure that it is a consistent part of their practice. The protocol also helps to convince them that by working toward the Standards of Accomplished Teaching, they will improve the quality of the learning opportunities they provide their students. Candidates report that whether the assessors give them a passing score or not, the experience of being guided through this critical reflection exercise has improved the quality of their teaching.

Part I of this book uses research to explain why National Board Certification will have a greater impact both on the individual teacher's practice as well as on the culture of teaching if it is pursued in groups. The following toolkit is written to provide members of candidate groups and those who are working to support them with a variety of specific and practical strategies that will aid candidates in improving the quality of their teaching as they work to become identified as accomplished teachers through National Board Certification. These activities will not provide tricks on how to pass this assessment; they will connect candidate groups with strategies for how to effectively and collaboratively experience professional growth from the process. They will help teachers to improve the quality of their teaching.

Forming candidate groups may be easier in some areas than others. In some areas school districts, university partners, the state department of education or professional development collaboratives are educating teachers about National Board Certification and supporting them to work in groups. These agencies may provide a facilitator (an NBCT or other knowledgeable educator) who is trained to support the candidates through the intellectual, emotional and logistical challenges they will face, and they may provide meeting space, portfolio development materials, and access to equipment. In other areas where the initiative to pursue certification comes from teachers, teachers have to form their own groups and find their own resources be it in their schools, in their regions or online. These teachers may find that the National Board Web site is a good place to look for collaborative partners; the Directory of NBCTs can be used to contact NBCTs in their own area who may know of other candidates, potential resources, or experienced facilitators.

So…

After candidates have…

1.   formed a small **group** of teachers to work with,

2.   obtained and examined a copy of the **Standards for Accomplished Teaching** for your certificate area, and

3.   submitted the candidate **registration** online…

the group is ready to begin!

The National Board Certification timeline is dependent upon the fee payment schedule. That is, the portfolio due dates and assessment center testing windows are triggered by the dates on which candidate fees are received by NBPTS. Candidates can begin to work as soon as they obtain the portfolio development materials (now provided to registered candidates on CD-ROM).

Veteran NBCTs fondly refer to these materials as "The Box" due to the fact that these materials, which used to be provided in hard copy, were much weightier than anyone expected (in more ways than one) and the actual cardboard carton they came in developed a mystique because it had to be guarded so that the portfolio could be returned in it months later. As NBPTS makes moves toward online submissions and scoring, the mystique of The Box may fade.

Today, all of the materials candidates need to begin are in fact publicly available for download from the "Certificate Knowledge Center," which can be found in the Candidate Resource Center of the NBPTS Web site. This means that candidates do not need to wait for "The Box" to begin their work. They can plan and prepare as soon as they make the commitment to take on National Board Certification (see Figure 3.1).

Figure 3.1 **Candidacy Timeline**			
Stage I	Stage II	Stage III	Stage IV*
Need the **Standards** for the appropriate certificate area and a copy of the **Certificate Overview**	Need the **Portfolio Instructions**	Need the **Scoring Guides** and collected **student work samples/ videotaped lessons**	Need the **Assessment Center Information**
These activities can begin any time before the candidacy year. Candidates do not need to be working with the class they plan to document.	These activities are meant to be conducted as candidates are planning out their portfolio development strategy. They need to know their teaching assignment and curriculum, but do not necessarily need to be teaching.	These activities are meant to be conducted while candidates are teaching. They are developing and finishing their portfolio entries.	These activities are meant to be conducted in preparation for the assessment center test. *The test may be taken before, during, or after the portfolio development, thus stage IV may fall before stage II or III. Candidates set their own test dates.

The **Standards, Certificate Overviews, Portfolio Instructions, Scoring Guides,** and **Assessment Center Information** are all available for download in the "Certificate Knowledge Center" of the Candidate Resource Center on the NBPTS Web site. <www.nbpts.org> These materials are also provided on CD-ROM in "The Box" upon payment of the initial deposit, and hard copies can be requested directly from the National Board. <1-800-22-TEACH>

Clarification of Terms

Throughout this section the term "standards" is used to mean any one of the sets of *Standards for Accomplished Teaching* as published by the National Board for Professional Teaching Standards. As of 2002, standards have been developed in 31 areas, reflecting different subjects and developmental levels.

The term "portfolio entry directions" or "PED binder" refers to the portfolio development instructions, which can be obtained in three ways. If candidates download them from the NBPTS Web site or upload them from the CD-ROM, they will want to print them and place them in a three-ring binder. Candidates can also request hard copies directly from the National Board for Professional Teaching Standards.

The term "group," as referenced throughout this section, suggests two or more people.

It is helpful to have an NBCT or other noncandidate "facilitator" guide the work of the group. This facilitator should be prepared to serve candidates' intellectual, emotional, and logistical needs through their own expertise or through their knowledge of resources. Small groups of teachers who decide to work on National Board Certification without an external facilitator however will also find this section of the book useful. These groups should designate a facilitator from among themselves, a position that can rotate among the group members, because activities in this toolkit are written with a facilitator in mind.

Special note to group facilitators who are NBCTs . . .

National Board Certified Teachers who serve as candidate support facilitators have the advantage of knowing what the experience is like. You want to lend the voice of experience, to be there to support others as you wish you were supported, and to help others learn from your mistakes. Yet, there are two important words of caution.

1) There **is** such as thing as too much help. Be sure to download and carefully read the *Handbook for National Board Certified Teachers* which is accessible at http://www.nbpts.org/pdf/nbcts_handbook_2001.pdf. This publication clarifies the limits for being a candidate advocate and includes lots of other useful information for NBCTs.

2) NBCTs who were certified before 2001 must be keenly aware of potential misconceptions that you may have about the certification process. You must be aware that while much remains the same (for example, standards-based assessments, basic structure, Five Core Propositions), the current portfolios are very different from the ones you experienced. The new design is informed by psychometric review of 8 years of pilots and assessments and with the recognition that more evidence was being collected than was needed to determine if a teacher is able to practice at the level of the standards.

> Several of the Standards have been revised. The Standards are living documents, which will continue to be revisited and revised on a regular basis. When the Standards change, the assessment may need to be altered as well. (For example, recently released Standards have a stronger emphasis on technology, and the new assessment requirements will necessarily reflect this change.) Be sure to take the time to become familiar with the new Standards, taking special note of changes within your own certificate area.

(Six sets of Standards have been revised as of August 2001: EC/GEN, MC/GEN, EA/GEN, EA/ELA, AYA/Math, EAYA/Art.)

There are four portfolio entries (not six), and there are six assessment center exercises (not four) that focus on content (and not pedagogy). The directions have been reordered and streamlined. Details such as font sizes, video length, and assessment center restrictions have all been changed. Be sure to visit the NBPTS Web site and/or borrow a candidate's portfolio instructions to become familiar with the new entry directions and assessment center requirements before giving advice.

Candidates who come into the process now have their deadlines based on when payment is received. You need to be aware that the deadlines are not the same for all candidates, even if they are working on the same certificate.

An argument could be made that this is a higher-stakes situation for today's candidates because the public is more aware of National Board Certification, whereas prior to 2001 many teachers were able to do it in "secret." At the same time, new candidates are likely to receive less recognition as our numbers grow. Be respectful of their fears and concerns, and realize that the support group may need to continue to play an important role in supporting candidates after they complete the process.

Organization of the Candidate Support Activities

Candidate groups have different needs, different parameters, and different dynamics. This book has been organized into several strands that represent major areas in which candidates may need support. In this way, candidates may choose the activities from this resource which will best serve their individual needs and/or the style of the group.

The activity strands are as follows:

A. Establishing Trust within the Group

B. Recognizing Accomplished Teaching and Internalizing the Standards

C. Management/Organization Strategies

D. Documented Accomplishments

E. Student Work-Based Entries

F. Video-Based Entries

G. Writing

H. Assessment Center Preparation

I. Continuing Candidates

As opposed to working through these activities in order, candidate groups are encouraged to consider their unique meeting schedule (weekly for 4 months? monthly for 1 year?) and their unique professional growth needs to determine the order in which areas will be addressed. Some groups know that the required writing tasks will be a challenge and will decide to begin there. Other groups recognize that managing and organizing the work will be a potential pitfall and will choose to start there. The activities in this collection are each prefaced by a table that will assist candidates or facilitators in identifying activities that will suit their needs.

Sample Table:

Title of Activity	
Group size	indicates the ideal group configuration for the activity
Relevant strands	indicates the related strands addressed by the activity
Materials	indicates any materials necessary beyond the candidates' standards
Timeline	indicates the stage during the candidacy year at which the activity is appropriate
Credit	indicates the contribution of a candidate support provider or other source

Figure 3.1

Matrix of Candidate Support Activities

Activity	A	B	C	D	E	F	G	H	I	Page
These Candidates, at This Time, in This Setting	X		X						X	44
Identifying Allies	X		X							44
Preparing Family and Colleagues	X									50
Why Are We Here?	X									52
Fears Activity	X		X						X	52
Meeting Warm-ups	X		X							53
Seeing Yourself in the Standards I		X	X	X	X	X	X		X	57
Seeing Yourself in the Standards II		X								57
Internalizing the Standards		X	X	X	X	X	X	X	X	58
The Vocabulary of Accomplished Practice		X					X	X	X	59
Examining the Rubric		X							X	61
The Right Stuff			X							65
Reading and Understanding Directions		X	X							66
Curriculum Mapping			X		X	X			X	69
Communications Log		X		X						71
Documenting Your Accomplishments		X		X						72
Making Good Choices		X		X					X	74
Sample Accomplishments				X					X	74
Choosing Student Work Samples					X		X		X	80
Knowledge of Students					X		X			82
Knowledge of Your Subjects					X			X		84
Taping Early and Often			X			X				86
Tape Critique		X				X	X			86
Distinguishing between the Three Types of Writing							X		X	90
Reflection	X						X			92
Getting Useful Feedback		X					X		X	93
Clear, Consistent, and Convincing Evidence		X					X			95
Assessment Center Interface								X		103
Study Groups		X						X		103
Study Planning								X		104

X indicates that the activity addresses this strand.

Toolkit for Candidate Groups

Activities Organized by Strand

Strand A

Establishing Trust within the Group

Teaching can be a very private profession. We rarely take the opportunity to talk with other adults about what goes on in our classrooms and when we do, we are challenging the norms of traditional teaching culture. Yet research tells us that good seeds grow in strong cultures.[1] A National Board Certification candidate support group must nurture a culture of collaboration so that teachers working in the group will benefit from sharing their classroom reflections, critiquing one another's videos, and analyzing their classroom successes and failures together. Teachers should not expect that breaking deeply rooted cultural norms will be easy to do. It will require that facilitators and candidates take time to establish trust among the members of their group.

Following are some activity suggestions that will help to establish and maintain the trust that candidate group members need to support one another's learning.

These Candidates, at This Time, in This Setting	
Group size	N/A
Relevant strands	A, C, I
Materials	Copies of "Candidate Database" and "Candidate Notes"
Timeline	I

The National Board Certification process asks teachers to regularly assess and reflect on how appropriate their choices are for "these students, at this time, and in this setting." Facilitators might do well to think about the group in the same way. What is it that these candidates need, at this time, in this setting? In order for the group to do this, facilitators and candidates must take time to learn about one another.

As facilitators and candidates, everyone should be sure to take the time to learn about the personal lives, professional settings, time limitations, family commitments, and so on, of the candidates you are working with by getting to know them. This can only be done if the lines of communication are open. You will find that some of the activities included in this strand are helpful in opening up communication among the group members; you may also find that true connections require individual contact (phone, e-mail, person-to-person).

You should establish a database of information on the candidates in the group so that everyone will be able to keep track of who the candidates are, what they need at this time, in their particular setting. The templates in figure 3.2 may be useful in collecting this data.

Be sure copies of the completed "Candidate Database" information sheet are distributed to all candidates in the group; it will help you to be a support to one another between seminar sessions.

Identifying Allies	
Group size	Whole group, then individual reflection
Relevant strands	A, C
Materials	"Types of Support" and "Identifying Allies" copies (1 on overhead)
Timeline	I

Regardless of how much one tries to warn them, many candidates find the National Board Certification process to be more challenging and time consuming than they expected. It is important for candidates to identify the friends, family, and colleagues around them who will be able to serve as allies as they begin to face challenges.(See Figure 3.3).

In preparation for this activity, facilitators should review the handout "Types of Support," which provides a useful structure for thinking about

Figure 3.2. Candidate Database

Name	Address	Phone #, E-Mail	Certificate Area	School/District

Figure 3.3. Candidate Notes

Name	Why Doing This/Why Now	Fears	Needs

the types of support that are required throughout the National Board process (see Figure 3.4). Remember that a candidate support group cannot provide *all* types of support for all candidates. (If you are a noncandidate facilitator, review the listed questions before you begin working with your group; then when you meet with your candidates, be honest with them about what kinds of support you can and cannot provide.)

Use the graphic worksheet "Identifying Allies" (see Figure 3.5) as an overhead and lead a discussion about the three types of support as a group. Brainstorm the kinds of people who might provide it (spouses, professors, principals, neighbors, and so on.) Next, candidates should be given a blank worksheet and time to fill in the names of specific people.

While this activity may seem simple, it is surprising how effectively it helps to remind candidates that they live next door to a writing tutor, that their cousin's husband has a videotaping business, or that a former professor may be willing to assist them. This activity will help candidates identify and make effective use of the resources around them, and maybe even share them with each other.

NBCTs as Allies

There are a number of ways to connect directly with NBCTs who may be willing to serve as allies. The NBPT's Web site hosts a directory of NBCTs, which can be sorted by state or certificate area. You can use this list to make contact with NBCTs via e-mail or through their schools. In addition, there are numerous listservs that one may join (see Appendix D); however, these are less often frequented by NBCTs.

You should think about the type of support that you are seeking before you contact an NBCT and be clear about it in your communication. Are you looking for someone with whom to discuss the Standards? Are you looking for someone who can help you increase your knowledge and skills in an area to help you meet the Standards? Are you looking for someone who can share your joy when you make a great video? These questions might help you to consider whether you need a local NBCT with whom you can meet in person versus an online NBCT with whom you can exchange e-mail.

You should also be aware that NBCTs are limited in the forms of support they can provide. These limits are clearly spelled out in the *Handbook for National Board Certified Teachers,* which is accessible at http://www.nbpts.org/pdf/nbcts_handbook_2001.pdf.

☞ **Remember**: Just because a teacher is certified doesn't mean she speaks for the Board! If you have questions about portfolio entry directions or submission requirements, they are best addressed by the National Board itself through the "Frequently Asked Questions" page of the Web site or by calling 1-800-22-TEACH.

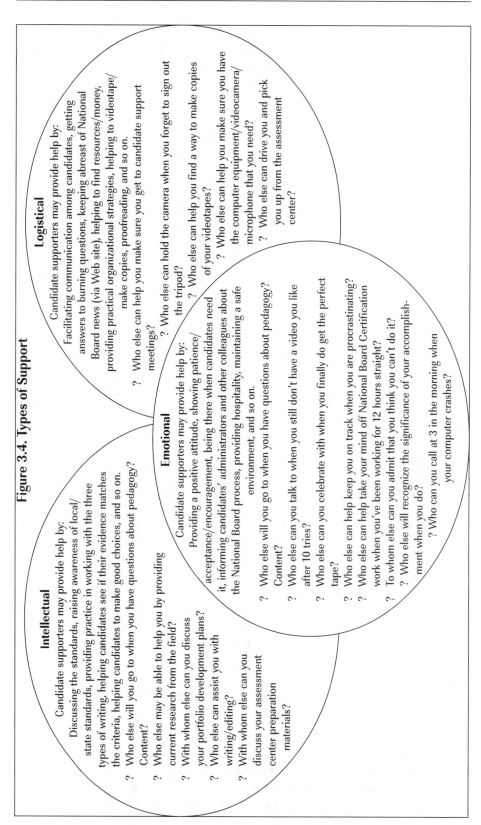

Figure 3.4. Types of Support

Intellectual

Candidate supporters may provide help by:
Discussing the standards, raising awareness of local/ state standards, providing practice in working with the three types of writing, helping candidates see if their evidence matches the criteria, helping candidates to make good choices, and so on.

? Who else will you go to when you have questions about pedagogy? Content?

? Who else may be able to help you by providing current research from the field?

? With whom else can you discuss your portfolio development plans?

? Who else can assist you with writing/editing?

? With whom else can you discuss your assessment center preparation materials?

Logistical

Candidate supporters may provide help by:
Facilitating communication among candidates, getting answers to burning questions, keeping abreast of National Board news (via Web site), helping to find resources/money, providing practical organizational strategies, helping to videotape/ make copies, proofreading, and so on.

? Who else can help you make sure you get to candidate support meetings?

? Who else can hold the camera when you forget to sign out the tripod?

? Who else can help you find a way to make copies of your videotapes?

? Who else can help you make sure you have the computer equipment/videocamera/ microphone that you need?

? Who else can drive you and pick you up from the assessment center?

Emotional

Candidate supporters may provide help by:
Providing a positive attitude, showing patience/ acceptance/encouragement, being there when candidates need it, informing candidates' administrators and other colleagues about the National Board process, providing hospitality, maintaining a safe environment, and so on.

? Who else will you go to when you have questions about pedagogy? Content?

? Who else can you talk to when you still don't have a video you like after 10 tries?

? Who else can you celebrate with when you finally do get the perfect tape?

? Who else can help keep you on track when you are procrastinating?

? Who else can help take your mind off National Board Certification work when you've been working for 12 hours straight?

? To whom else can you admit that you think you can't do it?

? Who else will recognize the significance of your accomplishment when you do?

? Who can you call at 3 in the morning when your computer crashes?

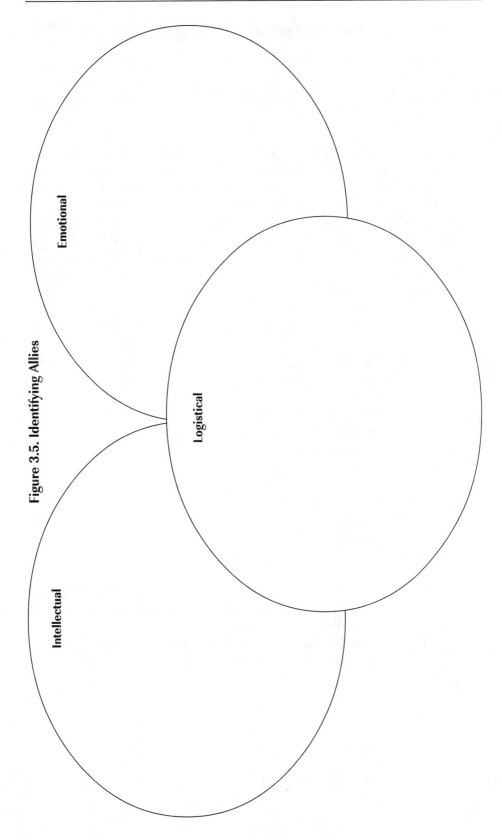

Figure 3.5. Identifying Allies

Preparing Family and Colleagues	
Group size	Whole group
Relevant strands	A
Materials	"Preparing Your Family and Colleagues"
Timeline	I

National Board Certification is a time-consuming, energy-sapping, mind-engulfing process that may take up to 3 years to complete. Various candidates have said that it is more work than a doctoral dissertation, higher pressure than an important job interview, more physically and mentally challenging than a marathon, and parallel in many ways to giving birth. Candidates who are not supported to handle this pressure in healthy ways have found themselves losing or gaining weight, restarting broken habits such as smoking or nail-biting, or even experiencing strained relationships with loved ones. Candidates must be prepared for the commitment they have made, and they need to work with family members, roommates, colleagues, and friends to help them make sure it will be a healthy growth experience.

Candidates should take time to carefully consider the potential impact of their decision on those close to them.

Would you enter a doctoral program,
    take on a new job with demanding hours,
        begin training for a marathon or
            plan to add a new baby to the family...
                without telling your...
...spouse/partner, roommate?
...parents, children?
...colleagues, boss?
...friends?

We all have a different relationship, sense of responsibility, and commitment to those around us. Only you can decide the extent to which you need to involve others in your decision.

The chart in Figure 3.6 may be helpful as you consider laying plans to make sure your candidacy experience is a healthy one.

Figure 3.6. Preparing Your Family and Colleagues

Family	Colleagues
Spouse/Partner/Roommate: • Consider whether you should make the decision together. • Let them know that they can expect this to be a considerable demand on your time and energy. • Set aside quality time by scheduling it into your calendar. • Discuss impact on traditions, vacation plans, and so on. • Consider need for additional resources (computer, child care, and so on). • Negotiate other commitments; decide together which commitments will have to go. • Thank them in advance for their patience. **Children:** • Tell them about the commitment you have made and why you want to do it. • Tell them that you will have a lot of homework to do just like they do. • Use this as an opportunity to model life-long learning, striving for excellence, and commitment.	**Colleagues:** • Carefully consider the colleagues with whom you work most closely and try to identify at least one colleague in your building who can be an ally. Take time out of school to cultivate this friendship: Explain to them what you are doing, the extent of what it entails, and your feelings about it. • Encourage them to learn more through the NBPTS Web site. • Let team teachers know what to expect: You will need them to be respectful of your videotaping (Can they help?); you will need space in the room to archive materials; you may be tired, distracted, or even absent at times. **Principals:** • Plan a meeting to explain that you are a candidate for National Board Certification and be clear about why you are doing it. • Work together to decide if and how National Board Certification might be introduced to the school staff. (Often the candidate is not the best person to do this. The principal can arrange to bring in an outside speaker.) • Be clear that your work as a candidate may limit your involvement in other school-based initiatives this year, but will strengthen your teaching and build your capacity as a resource in the future. • Discuss how your portfolio permission requirements for videotaping and student work align with school and in-district permission policies.

Resources

Ask family and colleagues to visit the NBPTS Web site: **www.nbpts.org.** Call the NBPTS to order materials it has created for these purposes. Provide copies of articles that have been published about National Board Certification: Order a copy of the *Harvard Education Letter,* March/April 2002, vol. 18, no. 2.(1-800-513-0763). Look for information and articles about National Board Certification on the NEA and AFT Web sites: www.nea.org or www.aft.org. Use a search engine to identify current articles.

Why Are We Here?	
Group size	Whole group
Relevant strands	A
Materials	None
Timeline	I

At the very first candidate meeting, candidates should, of course, introduce themselves. In order to help begin the network of trust and understanding, participants should, in addition to saying their names, describe their teaching settings and talk about why they have made the decision to pursue National Board Certification. It is not a decision to be taken lightly; yet at this early stage in the process, most candidates have likely never had to explain their reasons to anyone before. Since colleagues and critics will certainly ask this question in the future, this is a safe environment where candidates can develop an articulate answer. The sharing of such an intensely personal and professional commitment is a bonding experience for the candidates.

Fears Activity	
Group size	Whole group
Relevant strands	A, C, I
Materials	None
Timeline	I

After candidates get to know one another and really understand the blueprint of the National Board process, it is useful to have candidates brainstorm some of the fears they have about the process. This can allow the seminar facilitator to make informed decisions about what "these candidates need, at this time, in this setting" and can also enable candidates with similar fears to bond and support one another.

Some of the fears they are likely to identify are
- Time away from family
- Fear of embarrassment/failure
- Exposure/being in the public arena
- Procrastination
- Other job responsibilities
- Lack of control over the process
- Technical problems
- Nonmastery of video skills, writing skills, word processing skills, and so on
- Feeling overpowered by the size of the project
- Keeping up with day-to-day demands of teaching
- Being challenged as an agent of change
- Making choices
- Fear of the unknown

The group facilitator should be sure to take notes as participants share, in order that he or she will be able to use this information to serve candidates' needs throughout the seminar. [Suggestion: Use the "Candidate Notes" worksheet presented earlier in this section in Figure 3.3.] Some of the candidates' fears will be issues that can be addressed by the group; others will be issues that must be left entirely to the candidate. Identifying and articulating these fears help everyone. If you are a noncandidate facilitator, be clear with your candidates about how you can assist them and do not make any promises that you cannot keep.

Meeting Warm-ups	
Group size	Whole group
Relevant strands	A, C
Materials	Chart paper/markers
Timeline	I, II, III, IV

Once trust is established in the group, it needs to be maintained. As the deadlines approach, it is easy for groups to fall into a pattern of getting right down to business; however, it is especially important that candidates trust each other when they are in the process of giving each other honest and frank feedback.

Make time at the beginning of each session for candidates to share something about themselves. Following are some suggestions for topics to discuss at the beginning of each meeting:

- **Predict the future:** What kinds of problems is this going to cause in your life? What will the benefits be? What kinds of new roles will you seek after certification?

- **What's for dinner:** What are some easy ways to make sure your family does get fed and properly cared for despite the fact that you have no time?

- **Teacher who made an impression on you:** Tell about a favorite teacher you had and try to identify which of the National Board's Five Core Propositions that teacher embodies.

- **Learning despite the teacher:** Tell about a bad experience you had with a teacher and about how coping with him or her helped you to learn a lesson or skill.

- **Share time management strategies:** How will you/how do you set aside time to get everything done? What is your plan?

- **Favorite book:** What is a favorite book from your childhood? What is your favorite education-related book?

- **Great moment from the classroom:** Tell about your greatest moment in the classroom and why you are proud of it.

- **Worst moment in the classroom:** Let's laugh together about a failed lesson.

- **Critical friends:** Brainstorm/share who your allies are in this process (family, colleagues, and so on) Who do you want to draw in as an ally?

- **Dilemmas:** Suggest solutions to given scenarios: "A peer candidate approaches you with a math lesson she or he thought was the best. You don't see how it meets the Standards. How do you tell him or her? How would you want to be told?" (Take notes on candidate responses. They may come in handy down the line!)

You will want to vary the structure of these discussions. Try brainstorming as a group on chart paper, sharing in small groups or pairs and then reporting back to the group, or having 5 minutes of quiet written reflection and then sharing, and so on.

Strand B

Recognizing Accomplished Teaching and Internalizing the Standards

Many teachers assume that because they are teaching their students are learning. The National Board Certification process challenges this assumption by requiring teachers to provide evidence of the impact of their teaching on their students. Research tells us that effective professional development must be job-embedded, as close to the teaching as possible. By asking teachers to provide a rationale for all of their teaching choices, to defend why those choices are appropriate for their students, and to reflect on the impact of those choices on student learning, the National Board has established a highly effective protocol that can support teachers in developing this habit of inquiry, which is focused directly on the teaching moment.

When teachers work together to examine their assumptions and to help one another look critically and objectively at their previously private practice, they are better able to make lasting improvements in their practice. But what kind of changes will lead to improvement? What does accomplished teaching look like?

In the same way that houses with the same substructure may each present a different façade, an Architecture of Accomplished Teaching is common to all teaching practice and looks different at each certificate level.[2] All accomplished teachers focus their teaching choices on the needs of "these students, at this time, in this setting," yet elementary school teachers use different knowledge, skills, and dispositions to impact student learning than accomplished secondary music teachers do. For this reason, the National Board has gathered together educators at each grade level and subject area to develop Standards. The Standards help teachers know exactly what accomplished teaching looks like at their own grade level and in their own subject area.

During the process of portfolio development, teachers are identifying, analyzing, and reflecting on evidence of the Standards in their own practice. This process of researching one's own teaching helps teachers to identify their own strengths, while aiding them to recognize adjustments they can make to meet the Standard. Since the scoring rubric that is used to assess the work that candidates submit (included in the "Scoring Guide") is based entirely on the Standards, teachers must align their practice to these Standards to achieve certification. Some may manage to do this temporarily—if their aim is merely to become certified. Others take the time to reflect on how aligning their practice to these standards will help them to develop habits of inquiry that will improve the impact of their teaching on their students. The Standards are the key to achieving improvement, not merely change. **It is essential, therefore, that candidates read, understand, live, and breathe the Standards.**

Following are activities that will assist candidates in recognizing and developing the standards of accomplished teaching in their own practice.

Seeing Yourself in the Standards I	
Group size	Individual
Relevant strands	B, C, D, E, F, G, I
Materials	Standards, highlighter marker
Timeline	I

As soon as candidates begin considering the commitment to take on National Board Certification, they should obtain a copy of the Standards that apply to their teaching area. (A copy of the Standards can be downloaded from the NBPTS Web site, printed from the CD-ROM provided in The Box, or ordered directly from the National Board by calling 1-800-22-TEACH.)

Upon an initial reading of the Standards, candidates will recognize their own practice in what they are reading. They will think, "That reminds me of the way I do _____," or "That is very important to me because _____." They may even think, "I haven't tried that. Maybe I could incorporate that into my practice by _____." Candidates should read through the Standards carefully while highlighting portions that they feel are important to them, and use the ample margins to make notes of specific examples of how they see their own practice reflected in the Standards. It is recommended that they also take note of changes they would like to make to improve their practice.

This exercise is an important preliminary exercise because it will assist the candidate in identifying areas of strength and weakness. This annotated copy of the Standards will also become a useful resource when the candidicate begins making choices in developing the portfolio entries because it will serve as a log of his or her own activities and routines that meet the Standards.

Seeing Yourself in the Standards II	
Group size	Cert-specific groups, any size
Relevant strands	B
Materials	Standards
Timeline	I, II

Teaching is an intuitive activity for many teachers; many of the things teachers do without thinking are effective parts of their practice. This exercise helps candidates become aware of some of these practices. It helps them to think about the Standards from different angles and perspectives.

After individual candidates have had a chance to "see themselves" in the Standards, they should work in pairs or groups to share their reflections. To do this, each group should choose a particular Standard. Candidates within the group will then take turns to describe specific examples of the ways in which that Standard is reflected in their practice. This gives candidates a chance to share strategies and/or approaches and opens their minds to different applications and interpretations of the Standards. During this activity, candidates invariably think of additional examples of places where they see the Standards reflected in their own practices. They can then add these examples to the notes they have taken in the margins of their own copy of the Standards.

Internalizing the Standards	
Group size	Small group/pair discussion and individual strategies provided
Relevant strands	B, C, D, E, F, G, H, I
Materials	Standards, highlighter marker
Timeline	I

The Standards were created by committees of teachers, professors, and other experts in the field who were charged with articulating what the Five Core Propositions would look like when practiced by accomplished teachers at a given developmental level and subject area. Their validity comes from the public scrutiny of hundreds of stakeholders during the open comment period of their development, and they are kept current on a 5-year revision cycle. Whether or not these Standards for accomplished teaching can be considered empirically-based is a matter of debate for some. They are grounded in the experience of thousands of years of classroom teaching by hundreds of teachers—a source of knowledge not accepted by traditional science.

It is essential for teachers who want to improve the quality of their teaching to know what quality teaching—or accomplished teaching—looks like. The Standards for Accomplished Teaching provide that benchmark. It is not enough for candidates to read through the Standards and nod their heads in agreement. Candidate group facilitators must create multiple and varied opportunities for candidates to engage with the Standards for Accomplished Teaching, to understand them, and to challenge them.

The following activities have assisted candidates in internalizing the Standards. By working in pairs or small groups, candidates will benefit from multiple perspectives and will challenge one another's thinking.

Discussion Activities

Hundreds of teachers from your certificate area have agreed that this is what accomplished teaching looks like. Do you agree? What's unnecessary? What's missing? Which of the given Standards is most/least important and why?

Compare the Standards to the Scoring Rubric (level 4) or the "How Will

My Response Be Scored?" section of any one of the portfolio entries. With the two documents side-by-side, compare the language.

Choose a course and/or unit you have taught recently. Which of the Standards were reflected in that unit? Use your plan book or unit notes to help you reflect on the unit lesson by lesson. Are there Standards that could have been incorporated? What would the implications have been on teaching and learning?

Simple Strategies

The short version of the Standards—located in the front of your Standards booklet—can be very useful:

- Make several copies: Put one in your plan book, post one at school, post one at home, and so on.
- Write them on individual post-its and post them around your desk and/or computer.
- Memorize them.
- Make four copies, one for each portfolio entry. Highlight the Standards that apply to each entry and use it as a cover sheet for your entry drafts.

The full-length version of the Standards provides vivid descriptions of what accomplished teaching looks like:

- Audiotape them and listen to them in the car; this is a good time to reflect on them.
- Give them color codes or symbols so that you will be able to refer to them easily in your plan book, in the margins of your entry drafts, and so on.
- Rewrite them in your own words.

The Vocabulary of Accomplished Practice	
Group size	Small groups
Relevant strands	B, G, H, I
Materials	Dictionary, Standards, portfolio entry directions, "Vocabulary of Accomplished Practice" handout
Timeline	I, II, III

Candidates will find that certain words and phrases are repeated frequently throughout the National Board materials. These words and phrases pop up throughout the Standards, the portfolio entry directions, and the rubrics in the Scoring Guides. Figure 3.7 provides a collection of these words and phrases—"The Vocabulary of Accomplished Practice"—that can help teachers articulate the complicated processes of teaching and learning, demonstrate the tacit knowledge they hold, and put words to the effective practices they engage in so intuitively.

These words and phrases can be useful in a variety of ways. Candidates can discuss them in small groups, they can explore various interpretations of their meanings, and they can practice using them to develop increased facility with this rhetoric. When teachers are able to speak and write articulately and accurately about their teaching practices, they stand to gain more from their analysis and reflection of that teaching; one cannot analyze or reflect on what one cannot see. When teachers expose their practice by getting it out there in words, they will be better able to look at it from all sides, to analyze it critically, and reflect on it thoughtfully. Empowered with professional rhetoric, these teachers will also stand to make a larger contribution to the profession because they will be able to speak out and write and share the wisdom of their practice with various audiences.

Candidates might make use of this list in a number of ways:

- Group facilitators can select key terms for which candidates can develop their own definitions. Candidates can then discuss and debate their definitions with one another.

- A facilitator might present a group of related words and have candidates work in groups to explore their relative meanings.

- Candidates might also make a game of the task of hunting for a certain word or phrase in the Standards and portfolio directions, then comparing the different ways the term is applied throughout the literature. Similarly candidates can choose a word or phrase, then look for synonyms throughout the literature.

- Candidates can look for these words in the writing samples provided in Strand G.

- Candidates should think about their own content-, age-, and developmental-related vocabulary too. They can work with others in the same certificate area to develop their own certificate-specific lists.

☞   **Warning!** Good writing does not depend on jargon! Candidates should take care to learn what the terms mean and use them appropriately.

☞   **Also** Note that the "Getting Started" section of the portfolio instructions includes "Part 2: Glossary of Portfolio-Related Terms." This glossary provides logistical definitions for terms used in the portfolio directions, whereas the terms in the provided table are phrases used repeatedly throughout National Board work, which may be open to interpretation.

Figure 3.7. The Vocabulary of Accomplished Practice

terms related to learning and teaching... accomplished teaching standards "for these students, at this time, in this setting" multiple paths to learning high expectations for all students instructional purpose learning goals maximum learning high and worthwhile/realistic/appropriate goals instructional repertoire student performance managing and monitoring student learning	*an accomplished teacher should...* adjust instruction at critical points evaluate on the basis of "well-articulated criteria" maintain a disciplined learning environment provide "opportunity for meaningful participation" promote student interaction and reflection measure student growth shape instruction provide instructive feedback
loaded verbs... describe analyze explain evaluate reflect	*terms of reflection...* "next steps" for the students implications for future teaching lifelong learning reflective practice responsive to students' needs and developmental levels
loaded adjectives... appropriate specific equitable sound/principled (judgments) relevant (principles and theories) welcoming, safe, and challenging (learning environment) deep and broad (understanding) clear, convincing, and consistent (evidence)	*terms from Documented Accomplishments...* valuing members of the community enhance professionalism conscious and deliberate professional development two-way dialogue valued partners in education impact on student learning learning community broader community

Examining the Rubric	
Group size	Pairs/small groups then whole group
Relevant strands	B, I
Materials	Copies of all 4 levels of the scoring rubric for one entry, highlighter markers, chart paper/markers, scored writing samples
Timeline	II, III
Credit	Adapted from NBPTS Facilitators' Institute by Al Bird, NBCT

Adapted with permission from the national Board for Professional Teaching Standards, Facilitator's Institute, July 1999. All right reserved.

Group facilitators will need a Scoring Guide to prepare for this activity. Facilitators should select in advance one portfolio entry that will be the focus of this work. If the members of the group are working on different certificate areas, select *Entry 4: Documented Accomplishments* for this activity since it is the most similar across certificate areas. Make a set of copies of all four levels of the scoring rubric for this entry for each candidate. These are available in the Scoring Guides, which can be accessed online.

Distribute copies of the rubrics to the candidates. Work together in pairs or small groups to highlight all of the adjectives in each of the four rubrics. Ask candidates to compare the language used in the rubrics and to take note of their observations.

Examining the Rubric
Sample observations chart

Levels 1 and 2	Levels 3 and 4
• Limited evidence; little or no evidence of teachers working with parents... • Descriptions, verification, and summary are consistent; may show imbalance	• Clear evidence; Clear, convincing and consistent, evidence of teachers working with parents... • Descriptions, verification, and summary are unrelated

Figure 3.8

Working as a whole group, use chart paper to record your observations in the format of a T-chart, with observations about the Level One and Level Two rubric in one column, and observations about the Level Three and Level Four rubric in the other. (See Figure 3.8). Direct candidates' attention specifically to the differences between the Level Three rubric and the Level Two rubric: This is the distinction between accomplished teaching (a passing score) and teaching that is not considered accomplished (a failing score). By analyzing together the difference between accomplished teaching and good teaching, teachers will more clearly understand what they need to do to improve the quality of their teaching to become accomplished teachers.

Next use this chart to examine writing samples. (You will need to obtain one from an NBCT or use the ones included with the activities in Strand G.) Find evidence in the writing that supports the Standards that apply to that entry. Candidates can use their own writing. NBCTs working with groups are reminded that the NBPTS owns the copyright on scored enteries, and grants NBCTs the right to use their performances for nonprofit, educational purposes. It is up to individual NBCTs to decide if they are comfortable sharing excerpts of their scored entries with candidates.

In this exercise, candidates are doing precisely what assessors do. Portfolio assessors look to determine if there is clear, convincing, and consistent evidence of the standard; they do not look for what is "wrong." (It is no surprise then that teachers who have not been National Board Certification candidates but have served as assessors report that the experience has a positive impact on their teaching and their students' learning.) The assessors' determination, however, merely tells us whether the teacher is able to practice at the level of the Standards, not whether he or she always does or always will. The power of this standards-based assessment is in the fact that the Standards are "high and worthwhile," they are worth working toward, and they help keep teachers focused on the impact of their teaching on their students. The changes that teachers make to align their practice with these Standards make them better teachers.

Strand C

Management/Organization Strategies

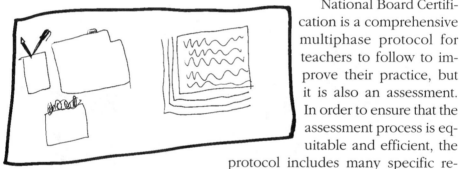

National Board Certification is a comprehensive multiphase protocol for teachers to follow to improve their practice, but it is also an assessment. In order to ensure that the assessment process is equitable and efficient, the protocol includes many specific requirements. There are page limits, font specifications, duplicate forms, time deadlines, and so on. Some of the requirements actually support the candidates' growth, as they support candidates to be clear and concise and to focus their attention on student learning, but many of them can seem petty and restrictive as well. They can distract teachers from the true matter at hand—improving their teaching practice.

The task of developing four portfolio entries simultaneously requires one to think about time management, workspace organization, organization of collected materials, technological considerations, and available resources. Effective management and organization systems will help candidates ensure that they are able to gather the evidence they need and to thoughtfully respond to the written prompts without undue time pressure.

Following are activities and strategies that have been effective for helping National Board Certification candidates to develop management and organization strategies that help them focus on professional growth, not format requirements.

The Right Stuff	
Group size	Whole group
Relevant strands	C
Materials	"The Right Stuff" handout and/or overhead
Timeline	I, II

Developing the portfolio is such a large organizational task that candidates will want to do everything possible to minimize the amount of time they spend shuffling papers, looking for things, and rewriting parts of entries. They will want to be able to put their hands on a particular piece of student work when they need it, be able to locate a certain Standard, and be able to work on developing the parts of the portfolio in an efficient and logical order.

To do this, they will need to have the right stuff. Recommendations are listed in Figure 3.9. You may want to review it with your group on an overhead, or just distribute copies. If your group is funded by a sponsor, ask if he or she can provide some of these items.

Figure 3.9. The Right Stuff

Developing the portfolio is such a large organizational task, you will want to do everything possible to minimize the amount of time you spend shuffling papers, looking for things, and rewriting parts of entries. You will want to be able to put your hands on a particular piece of student work when you need it, to be able to locate a certain Standard, and to be able to work on developing the parts of the portfolio in an efficient and logical order.
To do this, you will need to have the right stuff.

You will want to have

A 2″ three-ring binder, to hold your portfolio entry directions and your copy of the Standards.

A computer of your own, to allow you to work on your entries whenever you want and wherever you want. You will need to spend a significant amount of time on the computer; you don't want to have to wait until someone else is done, to sign up for time, or to be limited by the hours at a computer center/school. Remember, if you purchase one, it is tax-deductible! (It is a job-related expense.)

Several reams of paper, to print out endless drafts of your work. If a district is supporting your group, ask them to provide reams of paper. You might also seek out a local business that is willing to donate paper. They often are willing to donate their old letterhead, outdated reports, and so on, and you can print on the back.

Blank videotapes, to have on hand in your classroom. There is nothing worse than preparing to have a lesson taped and then realizing that you don't have a tape on hand.

Highlighters in several colors, to help you see at a glance where you are meeting standards and where you want to improve, to emphasize the suggestions in the "Making Good Choices" section that you will want to keep in mind, and so on.

---

cont.

Post-its in several sizes and colors, to help you keep track of entry progress, to keep track of reminders to collect signatures, student work, and other evidence, and so on.

A file drawer and hanging file folders, to store student work samples and videotapes in an organized way and to keep printouts of your portfolio entries as you develop them. You will want to have them available to show them to editors, and it is good to have a hard copy because you never know when your computer will decide to crash! Some candidates have found it useful to color code the folders by entry.

A traveling file box or expanding file folder, to tote student work samples between school/home in an organized way.

Back-up disks, to protect all of your precious files. Back up your files at a second location too (such as at school).

Other tips:

Keep your National Board work physically separate from schoolwork and other projects, and away from the work of others. You need your own workspace.

Use a Ghant chart, such as the one provided in "Getting Started" to help you plan out your work time.

Use a curriculum map to help you plan out your school year with all of your portfolio entry requirements factored in.

Save everything! Don't throw anything away until you have turned in your portfolio.

Reading and Understanding Directions	
Group size	Whole group, then Pairs or small groups
Relevant strands	C, B
Materials	Portfolio entry directions, "Understanding Entry Directions" worksheet and overhead, overhead markers
Timeline	II
Credit	Adapted from an exercise presented at the NBPTS Facilitators Institute

Adapted with permission from the National Board for Professional Teaching Standards, Facilitator's Institute, July 1999. All rights reserved.

The National Board Process requires a certain amount of jumping through hoops. Specific format specifications are necessary to maintain standard conditions for all candidates. But a breach of certain requirements may render an entire entry unscoreable. **It is important that candidates follow directions carefully!** The following activity has been effective to help ensure that candidates are able to understand and follow entry directions accurately. By encouraging candidates to think simultaneously about what is valued and what is required, these activities help candidates think about the places to look for evidence and about the kinds of artifacts that could be accepted as evidence.

Begin by having the group members turn to Entry 4 in their portfolio entry directions, because this entry is essentially the same for all certificates.

Part I

Ask candidates to work in pairs or small groups to examine the italicized passage on the first page of the chosen entry. This is an iteration of the Standards as they apply to this entry. Ask them to try to determine: "What will be valued in this entry?" based on the group's understanding of the italicized passage, and have them record their ideas in the left-hand column of Figure 3.10, "Understanding Entry Directions."

Figure 3.10

Understanding Entry Directions

Entry # ____

What will be valued in this entry?	What are candidates required to do?

When they are finished, ask the pairs to share their notes with the entire group. If you have a large group, record them on an overhead copy of the worksheet so that all can see. Reflect on your group's answers. Do you have a common understanding of what is valued and required?

Part II

Ask candidates to work in pairs or small groups again to examine the "What Do I Need to Do?" section in the same entry. They should carefully read and interpret the directions, then summarize their understanding in the right-hand column of Figure 3.10, "What are candidates required to do?"

When they are finished, have them all share, record, and reflect as before.

Part III

Explain that the bulleted list they have created on their "Understanding Entry Directions" page will be a useful reference tool, which they should insert into their PED Binder for later use. In a few months when their entries are drafted, they can use this page as a checklist to be sure that they have addressed what is valued and completed all requirements. Some candidates have even found this to be a useful cover sheet to attach to their entry drafts as they pass them on to readers who are not familiar with the process and its directions. Their readers can then give specific feedback about whether they feel there is clear, convincing, and consistent evidence of the Standards.

☞   **Note:** What are valued are, of course, the Standards, and the Scoring Guide also gives this same information in a different form (the rubric). However, this exercise helps candidates to thoroughly explore through discussion what the requirements mean, and enables them to restate the requirements in their own words.

Once you have gone through this exercise as a whole group, pairs or small groups of candidates who have the same certificate can choose another entry and replay the same activity on their own. You will need to provide additional copies of the "Understanding Entry Directions" worksheet.

☞   **Note of Caution to NBCTs:** Do not provide advice about the portfolio entry directions based on your own experience. The specifications may differ by year and by certificate area. Field candidates' questions about the PED Binder by having them look directly in the PED Binder for the current year or checking the NBPTS Web site.

Curriculum Mapping	
Group size	Individual
Relevant strands	C, E, F, I
Materials	Curriculum map template
Timeline	I, II

Three of the four portfolio entries are classroom-based, that is, candidates must provide evidence of the teaching and learning that occurs in their own classrooms for the current school year. Specific requirements vary from certificate to certificate; however, in general the evidence provided must represent the varied subjects and contexts in which you teach. For some certificates, student work samples must be obtained from two points in time to show progress; for others videotaped segments must show the introduction of a unit and a lesson from the end of the unit. These specifications require planning. Furthermore, by planning out the year, candidates will be able to work more efficiently, allowing more time for analysis and reflection, more time to make adjustments and align their practice to the Standards, and more time to improve their practice.

Candidates will do well to spend time prior to their candidacy year, if possible, mapping out the curriculum they plan to cover throughout the year.[3] In this way, they can coordinate the timing of the lessons they hope to feature. They can schedule activities that allow them to experiment with the Standards they need to develop, and they can be sure that they will have all of the evidence they need by the portfolio submission deadline.

The organizer form in Figure 3.11 has helped candidates create curriculum maps.

Figure 3.11. Curriculum Map

	September	October	November
General topic or unit			
Knowledge and skills			
Assessment Products and performances			

This sample shows 3 months of a year-long curriculum map. Use it as a model to create your own map.

Strand D

Documented Accomplishments

In the "Documented Accomplishments" portfolio entry, teachers are asked to provide evidence of their accomplishments as a learner, a leader, and a collaborator with families, colleagues, and the community. It is unique in that it is not a classroom-based entry, and it is the only portfolio entry in which work may be submitted from the past 5 years. It is also unique in that it focuses almost exclusively on the fifth Core Proposition: "Teachers are members of learning communities."

Some may question whether accomplished teachers have to be members of learning communities. Certainly a teacher working in the isolation of her own classroom might get strong student learning results. However, research reminds us that effective professional development must bring teachers together in collaborative problem solving, and it must be part of a comprehensive process. It creates a strong teaching culture in which students can expect that the adults are working together to surround them with rich learning opportunities, not competing to give them one good year. Since accomplished teachers are committed to students and their learning, they are concerned about improving the entire teaching and learning environment. They pursue learning opportunities, leadership roles, and collaborations that extend their influence beyond their own classroom to the home and the community of their students, and that extend beyond the current school year through work with colleagues and community organizations. They *must* be members of learning communities.

Many candidate groups find that this is a good portfolio entry with which to begin their work together for two reasons. Since the evidence is drawn from the past 5 years, candidate groups can begin their work on it before the busy school year begins. And since the entry directions are essentially the same for all certificate areas, group members from different certificate areas can support one another as they work on parallel tasks. This strategy allows teachers to feel more confident about the process of developing a portfolio entry before they begin work on the classroom-based entries.

Following are some activities that groups have used to assist candidates in preparing to document and reflect on their accomplishments.

 Beware! Many candidates find that reviewing their professional careers and looking for patterns to present in the interpretive summary causes them to begin thinking about the new roles they want to take on beyond candidacy.

Communications Log	
Group size	Whole group
Relevant strands	D, B
Materials	Chart paper, PED Binder/Entry 4
Timeline	II, III

Many candidates choose to include a log of the ongoing, interactive communications they have with parents. While the task of compiling this log can feel like a chore, candidates who keep these logs invariably notice patterns or omissions in their communication that they would not otherwise have perceived. They may notice that communication is ongoing but is not interactive (sending notes home and receiving no reply). They may notice a marked lack of communication with certain parents (such as the students who are doing fine), or they may perceive that there is a relationship between parent communication and student behavior (usually positive, but not always). Through analysis and reflection, teachers perceive these patterns and lay plans for improving their communication. In this way, documenting parent communication in a log helps improve the quality and usefulness of the communication.

The entire log will not be submitted with Entry IV. The certification process asks to see a sample of the frequency and variety of types of contact: phone, notes, hallway chats, and so on. It is also important that they show evidence of follow-up after contact. Candidates need to show evidence that all communication does not begin with them; they have made themselves available so that parents feel comfortable coming to them with questions or issues. The communication with parents must go in two directions. Sending home a weekly classroom newsletter is not two-way communication unless there is some way that it invites parents to respond to the newsletter and then they actually do it. The accomplishments listed in the log must show that they have gone above and beyond the contractual duties of a teacher.

Prepare a piece of chart paper with two columns as shown in Figure 3.12. Work as a group to brainstorm a list of as many forms of parent communication as you can and record them in the left-hand column. Next, read the italicized passage on the first page of the portfolio entry directions for Entry 4. These are the Standards as they apply to this entry. Then, use the right-hand column to explain why and/or how each form of communication you have brainstormed is interactive, ongoing, and has an impact on student learning.

Figure 3.12

Communications Log Sample Brainstorm Chart	
Parent communication	Impact on student learning
• Parent conference	• 2-way conversation, regularly scheduled, joint goal-setting helps student to see us as allies
• E-mail	• asynchronous communication but accommodates parent schedule and allows frequent communication, facilitates immediate response to student needs and concerns
• Newsletter • Run into parent in supermarket	

This exercise will help candidates see that listing certain forms of communication on their communication logs will be more effective than others for providing evidence of the relevant Standards. It will also help them to see the merits of various forms of communication, and encourage them to expand their repertoire.

Encourage candidates to start their logs early in the year and keep them all year long. At the end of the year, they will have a valuable source of data about their communication pattern, which chronicles one complete school year; they can use this log to make improvements next year.

Documenting Your Accomplishments	
Group size	Individual
Relevant strands	D, B
Materials	Professional development files
Timeline	I, II

This entry requires that teachers dig deeply into their file cabinets and their brains. They must recall all of the work they have done with families, all of the collaborations they have initiated with the community, all of the contributions they have made to the professional community as a facilitator or collaborator, and all of the opportunities they have pursued to develop themselves as a learner during the past 5 years. This is no small task.

While this work will most easily be accomplished at home where they have records of some of these events, candidates might work in groups to begin compiling their lists and thinking together about what should be included. The portfolio instructions state that accomplishments must go above and beyond the contractual requirements of teaching. Some discussion may be useful to gain a common understanding of what this means. (The system requires that parent conferences be at least 10 minutes, but mine are 1 hour; Parents' Night is not in the contract, but everyone does it; I took a course, but the school paid for it; and so on.)

The group can be useful in this process in other ways as well. When candidates share their lists of accomplishments, it invariably helps others to think of similar accomplishments they had forgotten. Groups are also a good place to think out loud. Have each candidate choose one accomplishment to describe to the whole group and explain its connection to student learning.

It is impossible to think of all of one's accomplishments in one sitting. In order to develop their lists of accomplishments further, candidates should show the list to several family members and colleagues, who will surely think of things they have missed. A look through home and school file cabinets will surely reveal several more items. Wait a week; candidates will think of still more accomplishments. Remind candidates that at this stage they should try to list absolutely everything. Candidates will need 2 to 4 weeks to come up with a complete list.

This will be the first time most teachers have collected this kind of information in one place. Questions such as the following will encourage candidates to examine their lists of accomplishments more closely:

How does it feel to view this list of accomplishments?

What patterns do you notice?

What do you think this list says about you?

What kinds of experiences do you wish were included?

The self-realization process instigated by this mountain of evidence is a powerful one. Teachers might recognize that they are drawn to certain types of learning experiences and begin to reflect on why this might be the case. They might notice that they have given the same workshop several times and commit themselves to expanding their repertoire. Others might notice that their collaborations with colleagues exist only outside of their school setting and make an effort to foster collaborations with their own teaching team. In fact, many teachers notice that they have no publications, but are inspired by the writing they have done for the National Board and want to try their hand at it. While the National Board Certification process requires candidates to select only a small sample of these accomplishments for analysis and reflection, candidates will benefit by pausing to consider the whole collection before paring it down. The evidence documents the accomplishments they have made as a learner, leader, and collaborator, within the profession, with parents, and with the community. What does this evidence suggest about next steps?

Making Good Choices	
Group size	Individual
Relevant strands	D, B, I
Materials	PED Binder/Entry 4, highlighter marker, paper/pencil, "Documented Accomplishments Categories" chart (from PED Binder)
Timeline	II, III

All entries in the PED Binder have a section entitled "Making Good Choices." Past candidates have found that this section is especially useful in preparing the Documented Accomplishments entry because there are so many choices to be made. Candidates should begin by reviewing this section with a highlighter in hand so that they are clear about what is important.

After candidates have compiled a reasonably complete list of accomplishments, ask them to revisit their highlighted notes from Entry 4's "Making Good Choices," and help them to use the guidance given there to begin the process of narrowing the list. Remind them to think about which of their accomplishments bring the learning home and have an impact on student learning. Also remind them to think about the story they will want to be able to tell in the summary for this entry. (Some candidates like to write this concluding reflective summary first.)

Once candidates have narrowed down their lists to several accomplishments, provide extra copies of the "Documented Accomplishments Categories" chart from their PED Binder in order that they can begin to spell out the rationale for their choices. After developing these charts, candidates can use one another to practice debating and defending their choices.

Sample Accomplishments	
Group size	All
Relevant strands	D, I
Materials	Copy of "Sample Documented Accomplishments"
Timeline	I, II

Many candidates have expressed an interest in knowing what kinds of accomplishments other candidates have documented. It is important to note that neither professional growth nor evidence of the Standards will come from examining a list of accomplishments alone. It is the analysis and reflection, taken together with the interpretive summary, which enable candidates and assessors alike to view accomplishments as evidence of the Standards.

Figure 3.13 lists some brief descriptions of some of the accomplishments that NBCTs have documented for their Documented Accomplishments entries. This list might be used as a resource for candidate support facilitators, or as a memory-jogger for candidates. It is meant to guide candidates in making good choices. It is *not*, of course, meant to be a comprehensive list of fail-proof accomplishments.

As you browse this list of accomplishments with candidates, you might brainstorm additional ways in which each accomplishment can be described as significant and think of additional forms of documentation that might be used to verify each accomplishment. The "Category" column refers to the areas in which candidates must demonstrate their work for this entry:

- Category I: Teacher working with students' families and community
- Category II: Teacher as leader/collaborator at local, state, or national level
- Category III: Teacher as learner

Figure 3.13. Sample Documented Accomplishments

Brief description of accomplishment	Significance	Documentation	Category
Communication log	Demonstrates variety and frequency of two-way communication Provides evidence of personalized instruction and follow-up	Original log	I
Presented a replicable teaching strategy at a conference	Increases student achievement for participants' students Demonstrates teacher leadership Demonstrates willingness to share effective strategies Demonstrates learning/growth through presentation development/reflection	Workshop evaluations Conference program	II, III
Mentoring new teachers/peers/high school students	Improves training of mentees and mentor Provides regular opportunity for reflection with others Models life-long learning Demonstrates collaboration	Letter from mentee Letter of verification Evaluation form Log of mentoring activity	II, III
Presenting in-service workshops	Shares effective practices Demonstrates teacher leadership Demonstrates willingness to share strategies Demonstrates learning/growth through presentation development/reflection	Agenda Workshop handouts Letter of verification from participants/ administrators Evaluation forms	II, III
Townwide strategic planning committee	Creates an impact on future townwide education plans Demonstrates participation in community life Provides an opportunity to learn from and collaborate with community Demonstrates teacher leadership	Project report (pamphlet) Letters of verification	I, II, III

cont.

Grant writing	Provides materials or programs which have a direct impact on student learning Demonstrates leadership/taking initiative to recognize need and identify resources	Cover page of grant Parent evaluations Photos Letters of verification	II
Organizing a schoolwide student post office	Motivates students to write/impact on student learning Fosters collaboration with community/ post office Increases parent communication Demonstrates leadership/taking initiative on behalf of whole school Attracts parent volunteers Shows teacher as learner through reflection throughout the year-long project	Letters from the post office Letters of verification Fliers for the event	I, II, III
Curriculum-writing/ mapping	Encourages reflection/learning about own practice Provides opportunity to adapt state standards Prepares students for state testing Demonstrates leadership in initiating teacher collaboration	Title page of curriculum Copy of curriculum map Letters from colleagues	II
Bringing parents into school: After the Prom Party	Motivates parents to become involved Establishes connections with community partners	Pictures Letters of verification Photo of T-shirt Newspaper article	I
Displaying student work in public library	Provides authentic audience for kids which is motivating and impacts student learning Provides opportunity for community to view the school	Photos of display Letter of verification from librarian Announcement of exhibit	I
Collaboration between two grades: building community curriculum for district	Impacts classroom community, which has an impact on student learning Creates common language for parents, students, teachers, staff Establishes collaboration with colleagues	Letters of verification Title page from published curriculum	II
Adopted a senior center	Impacts student learning through social competency goals and through opportunity for service Demonstrates collaboration with larger community Encourages parent involvement Impacts student learning through practice in letter-writing/thank you notes	Letters from seniors Newspaper article	I
Workshops for the School Committee on Reading	Increases funding for reading program—creating an impact on student learning Demonstrates teacher leadership through recognition of need and follow-through Encourages collaboration/new communication with school committee	Letters from principal and superintendent	I, II

cont.

Weekly newsletter	Increases parent involvement through attached parent response sheet Increases parent interaction with child through interactive elements Demonstrates ongoing, interactive communication with parents	Copy of newsletter with parent responses	I
Summer travel program, then producing a curriculum	Provides evidence of teacher as learner Demonstrates collaboration with colleagues through production of a curriculum which can be shared/also has an impact on student learning Increases empathy for students	Letter from professor Copy of final project/ curriculum	III
Writing for publications	Demonstrates teacher leadership/ engagement in field Impacts teacher as a learner/writer	Copy of publication	II, III

Strand E

Student Work-Based Entries

Teachers use a variety of sources to informally assess the effectiveness of their teaching. The frequency of insightful questions, the quiet hum of students writing, the din of rigorous discourse, and even a visit from a previous student all help teachers to know how they are doing. The student work-based entries are important opportunities for teachers to confront themselves more formally with evidence of the impact of their teaching on their students. The evidence they provide must demonstrate four of the National Board's Five Core Propositions.

- **Core Proposition #1:** As teachers demonstrate how their knowledge of students enables them to provide challenging learning experiences for those students, they show that that they "are committed to students and their learning."

- **Core Proposition #2:** As teachers make appropriate curricular choices and create meaningful learning experiences using current knowledge, effective practices and appropriate instructional resources, they show that they "know their subjects and how to teach them to students."

- **Core Propostition #3:** As teachers provide a rationale for their sequencing of instruction and their assessment methods, teachers demonstrate their ability to "manage and monitor student learning."

- **Core Proposition #4:** As teachers draw insightful conclusions from the collected evidence and from its analysis, and as they work to articulate the implications of those conclusions for teaching and learning, they "think systematically about their practice and learn from experience."

While teachers might also demonstrate that they are "members of learning communities" by connecting the curriculum to parent and community resources or by articulating what they themselves have learned from the students, these student work-based entries generally are not looking for the Standards that relate to this fifth Core Proposition.

These entries require that candidates make a tremendous number of important choices as they collect and write about their evidence. Candidates must decide which lessons and/or units to include, which students to feature, and which work samples to provide. All student work has something to tell us. In this process teachers must think like researchers and think about the kinds of data they will need to collect to provide a valid answer to their research question. They want to be able to provide clear, convincing, and consistent evidence that their teaching practice meets the Standards of Accomplished Teaching.

The following activities will help candidates as they conduct research through their student work-based entries.

☞ **Note:** The NBPTS has clear guidelines about obtaining permission to include student work and student images in the portfolio. This permission does not automatically extend to sharing student work and images among the members of your candidate group. You are responsible for determining what measures you should take to protect the rights and confidentiality of your students.

Choosing Student Work Samples	
Group size	Individual or pairs
Relevant strands	E, G, I
Materials	Student work samples, "For This Child…" work sheet
Timeline	II, III

Candidates are required to make many different choices throughout the process of developing the portfolio entries. They must choose which accomplishments to include and how many, which lessons and/or students to feature and through what evidence, which lessons to videotape and which segment of the tape to send, and so on. Those choices can make a big difference in how easy it will be for both assessors and candidates themselves to see the Standards in the portfolio work. While assessors are trained to detect evidence wherever it exists, the choices that the candidate makes can help assessors to see whether the candidate is clearly and consistently an accomplished practitioner. These same choices help make clear to candidates the impact of their teaching on their students.

Support facilitators can help candidates to recognize that the National Board process is an evaluation of accomplished teaching based on the teacher's performance, not the students' performance. The teacher's analysis and reflection of the professional decisions she makes to provide rich and appropriate learning opportunities for her students is what is most important. The Architecture of Accomplished Teaching reminds teachers that they need to know how the decisions they have made are appropriate for "these students, at this time, and in this setting."

Encourage candidates to collect work from at least three times the number of students they need for the student work-based entries. Having a large archive of student work provides the candidate with enough data to perceive patterns, to notice trends, and to thoughtfully select the student work that demonstrates his or her professional decision-making most vividly.

One good way to help candidates make good choices in selecting student work samples is to have them think about how the lesson is appropriate for that particular child, at that particular time, in that particular setting. To do this, have candidates select work samples from one assignment created by three different students. Have them use the worksheet in Figure 3.14, "For This Child, at This Time, in This Setting," or a journal to analyze the decisions they made in the process of assigning and evaluating those pieces of work.

Candidates can work together to help one another think critically about what each piece of work shows. They can do this by sharing their notes and explaining which student they feel best demonstrated the candidate's decision-making about the assignment. This conversation can help candidates to recall or realize some of the critical professional decisions that were made in the process of creating and assessing the work—decisions that are often made intuitively. They can then incorporate their reflections on this thinking into their writing.

Figure 3.14

For This Child, at This Time, in This Setting

Use this worksheet to help you work out your defense for the professional choices that you made in creating, selecting, and/or offering this assignment.

Brief description of the assignment:

Explain how this assignment is appropriate for...	...this child	...at this time	...in this setting
Student #1:			
Student #2:			
Student #3:			

Knowledge of Students	
Group size	Individual, then pairs
Relevant strands	E, G
Materials	Student work samples, student records, reference books
Timeline	II, III

The National Board's first Core Proposition tells us that all teachers should be "committed to students and their learning." The requirements and guiding question protocols for the student work-based entries in the portfolio entry directions help teachers take a systematic and scientific look at individual learners in their classrooms. Teachers become researchers of their students as they gather data on the individual students, form hypotheses about how each of them learns best, conduct experiments aimed at improving the students' learning, report on the conclusions, and provide implications for further study. This research begins with a knowledge of students.

Just as a doctor will take time to review a patient's medical history, examine and observe the patient, and conduct some exploratory examinations before making a diagnosis and prescribing a remedy, a teacher must take time to know his or her individual students well in order to accurately prescribe rich and appropriate instruction. Of course, teaching is complex—no doctor is asked to work with 30 patients with different symptoms all at once—and so teachers must become skilled at developing a knowledge of students efficiently and effectively.

This activity aims to help teachers develop a systematic strategy for developing their knowledge of students. Candidates should practice creating profiles by examining several individual students from a number of different angles. Following are some useful frames for thinking about the diversity that students bring to learning.

- One way to think about students is **developmentally**. Candidates should use their observations and assessments of students to think about the students' physical, cognitive, social, and emotional development levels. Any textbook on child development or a resource such as *Yardsticks: Children in the Classroom Ages 4–14* by Chip Wood (Northeast Foundation for Children, 1997) will be useful to candidates as they think about where their students are, relative to age-appropriate benchmarks and what their students need.

- Another way to think about students is through the lens of **multiple intelligences.** According to Howard Gardner's theory, there are at least eight different ways in which people are smart: linguistic, logical-mathematical, bodily-kinesthetic, visual-spatial, musical, naturalist, interpersonal, and intrapersonal. Candidates can think about these eight ways as they work to develop rich profiles of how their students are smart. For further reading, see: *Frames of Mind* by Howard Gardner (Basic Books, 1983).

- A student's developmental considerations and intelligences may influence **how the child learns best.** One useful theory is to think about the ways in which students might be visual, auditory, or kinesthetic learners. While these labels are not meant to be mutually exclusive, they provide another fresh angle from which to think about individual learners. For further reading, see: *Teaching Students to Read Through Their Individual Learning Styles* by Marie Carbo, Rita Dunn, and Kenneth Dunn (Prentice-Hall, 1986).

- It is important to have knowledge of students' **socio-cultural backgrounds.** The experiences, values, and traditions that students bring from home undoubtedly affect learning; they form the foundation of how students make meaning of the world. When teachers take time to become familiar with students' family structures, cultural traditions, and core values, they will be better equipped to help students use what they already know and believe to gain new knowledge.

- Teachers also glean important knowledge of students by learning what they do with **out-of-school time.** A periodic short interview or survey (with students and/or parents) can reveal interesting information about the child's interests, available resources, and talents, which teachers can use to enrich and increase learning opportunities.

- Lastly, teachers might want to consider gathering information about **students' past performance.** Cumulative record folders often have clues about student strengths or weaknesses, about hurdles the student has overcome, or about chronic problems that require attention. Candidates' research should include finding out what has worked—and what has not worked—for this student in prior learning settings so the candidate can use that knowledge to make informed decisions about new learning strategies.

By creating an archive of student profiles that focus their attention on these areas, teachers will have a rich source of data to use as they work to create challenging and appropriate learning opportunities for their students. They will also begin to build a repertoire of case studies, which can help inform and improve future instruction.

Candidates should be encouraged to use their student profile notes to create narratives and share them with partners in the group.

Knowledge of Your Subjects	
Group size	Individual or pairs
Relevant strands	E, H
Materials	Computer with Internet access
Timeline	II, III, IV

The National Board's second Core Proposition tells us that teachers should "know their subjects and how to teach those subjects to their students." Few would contest the claim that teachers need to know their content. Most would agree that teachers need to have some mastery of pedagogy. But some people forget how important it is to have content-related pedagogy and student-related pedagogy. Teachers need to know more than the content they are expected to teach; they need to know how to teach their subjects to their students.

Where can teachers go to learn more about effective strategies for teaching various subjects and about developmental considerations that are relevant to the students they teach?

- Candidates have **each other.** They can share their own knowledge and skills, recommend books and resources from their own personal libraries, and suggest conferences and workshops that will provide the needed learning.

- Candidates can use the **Web-based resources** listed in Appendix D to assist them in identifying the resources they need. Begin with AskERIC (a federally funded clearinghouse of education resources) at www.askeric.org. If you cannot find what you are looking for (or, more likely, you find too much), you can have an online expert help you. Next try professional associations from relevant fields. Check out their publication catalogues or conduct a keyword search. Also try searching the archives of professional periodicals such as Education Week, to which online access is free. You may find articles that will lead you to key authors or organizations in your area of interest.

- Candidates may be able to arrange access to **university** resources. With such an arrangement, candidates will be able to access hundreds of restricted-access online resources, academic journals and articles, and even faculty members with pertinent expertise.

Strand F

Video-Based Entries

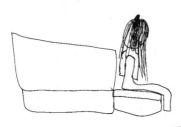 

While many of the strategies that support teachers to work with the student work-based entries will be useful here, the video-based entry has challenges of its own. This is the only opportunity for assessors to "visit" candidates' classrooms, to see student engagement, to hear candidates interact with students, and to experience the magic they create. Interestingly enough, for many candidates it is the only time they have ever "visited" their own classroom as well. It provides raw, undeniable, objective data which has more to say about the impact of their teaching on their students than most teachers would like to hear. This exercise challenges teachers even more than the other entries to break the norm of isolation, to expose their teaching practice, and to support one another in honest and collaborative problem solving. When candidates do work together to analyze these tapes in light of the Standards, to share interpretations, and to reflect on implications for future teaching, they learn exactly what they need to do to become better teachers.

But it all starts with having a tape. While illuminating, videotaping is also nerve-wracking. There are emotional, technological, and logistical considerations that must be taken into account. It can be scary for candidates to expose their previously private practice to one another for the first time. The trust you have established within your group will be important here. It can also be enormously frustrating to have a beautifully planned lesson interrupted by a fire drill, or to realize just as you are hitting your stride that you forgot to put a videotape in the camera.

Following are strategies that can help candidates focus on the evidence they are providing and not on the technological factors of the video-based entries. Appendix C, *A Guide to Videotaping*, has been provided to give candidates additional guidance regarding the more technical aspects of this entry.

Taping Early and Often	
Group size	N/A
Relevant strands	F, C
Materials	Copies of the "Video Log"
Timeline	II, III

One of the keys to making videotaping a valuable professional development experience is to start taping early, and to tape often. By taping early in the year, you will have the opportunity to work out the technical glitches, such as best angles, lighting, microphone placement, and so on, but you will also have baseline data to use as your teaching and your students' learning both develop. By taping often, you take the "showtime" factor out of the picture for yourself and for your students who have trouble acting natural in front of a camera. When you are ready to prepare your portfolio, you will have a large collection of data at your disposal which you can use to examine patterns in your teaching and from which to select authentic performances for your portfolio.

But when taping early and often, it is especially important to document your taped lessons; your data will be useless if it is buried in a mountain of unlabeled tapes. Documenting taped lessons means, at a minimum, labeling the tape with the date, time, and lesson. Ideally, it means keeping a log (see the log sample in Figure 3.15), in which you can jot down your perceptions and reflections about a lesson soon after it has occurred. It might be weeks or months before you come back to view the footage or decide how you plan to use it.

Tape Critique	
Group size	Any configuration
Relevant strands	F, G, B
Materials	Standards, videotaped lessons
Timeline	II, III
Credit	Activity contributed by Kevin Hart, NBCT

The purpose of this lesson is to familiarize candidates with taping techniques and issues. It will also serve to engage candidates in reflecting on their teaching and thinking about the different types of writing used by NBPTS candidates: descriptive, analytical, and reflective.

Part I

Candidates should read about the various portfolio taping requirements in their PED Binders, and about the different types of writing required (see Getting Started or activities in Strand G).

Figure 3.15. Video Log

Date: Time: Class:

Lesson:

Immediate impressions of the lesson:

How it was different than I had expected:

Changes I made in the lesson/choices I made midstream:

Lesson/student follow-up:

Part II

Show segments of videotaped teaching performances. They can be tapes produced for National Board Certification portfolios, or any other tapes. (Reminder: NBCTs can choose to use their materials for this educational nonprofit purpose.) Stop the tapes after **three** (not necessarily consecutive) intervals (about 7 to 10 minutes each).

1. **Discuss** the following:

    - What does the entry ask for?

    - Does the tape meet the general criteria for the entry?

2. After each of the three intervals of tape, ask the candidates to **write** a paragraph responding to one of the requirements (limit writing time to about 10 minutes per response).

    - Alternate the requirements so that the candidates **perform each of the three types of writing: descriptive, analytical, and reflective.**

    - Discuss the written responses ensuring that the candidates can both recognize when a particular type of writing is required and create that type of writing.

If you use veteran candidate performances, those candidates can elect to share their written commentary on those portions of the tape. The ensuing discussion will help all participants to see their own biases, assumptions, and values.

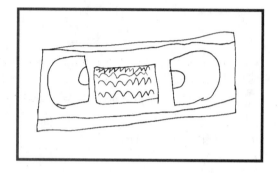

Strand G

Writing

Accomplished teaching is all about how the choices teachers make lead to student learning. Many teachers' teaching choices are grounded in tacit knowledge; the choices they make feel right and seem to work so they don't question them. Unless they have a reason to articulate their teaching choices, such as for a student teacher or an inquisitive parent, they are unlikely to do so. But the processes of teaching and learning are so complex that most teachers, including highly effective teachers, often find themselves at a loss for words to describe exactly how their teaching is leading to higher levels of student learning.

Accomplished teachers must be able to articulate their teaching choices. When teachers can articulate their teaching choices, they can think more objectively and critically about them; they can share their practice with others; and they can work collaboratively with colleagues, professional associations, researchers, and others to improve the quality of teaching.

In the National Board Certification process, candidates are challenged to put their practice into words. They must use writing effectively to demonstrate their knowledge of the students and the setting, to provide a rationale for the learning opportunities they choose to provide, to analyze their teaching and student performances, and to reflect on the implications for future teaching and learning. There are a number of ways candidate group members can build the skills they need to articulate their practice. By understanding the distinctions between descriptive, analytical, and reflective writing, they will be able to create portraits of their practice more clearly, completely, and efficiently and by serving as a critical audience for one another's oral and written practice, they will be supported to develop the rhetoric they need.

Following are activities that will help candidates become articulate about their teaching practice. See also "The Vocabulary of Accomplished Practice" activity in Strand B.

Distinguishing Between the Three Types of Writing	
Group size	Pairs/small groups
Relevant strands	G, I
Materials	"Three Types of Writing" handout
Timeline	I, II
Credit	Based on contributions from Betsy Sales, NBCT

The Getting Started section of the PED Binder includes an entire chapter dedicated to helping candidates understand the distinction between the three types of writing. Be sure to direct your candidates' attention to this section of the binder. They may take time on their own or in a group to review it.

Figure 3.16 may also assist you in helping your candidates understand the differences between these three types of writing.

Figure 3.16. Three Types of Writing

Description	Analysis	Reflection
• Retelling what happened • Allows outsider to see into your classroom • Accurate • Precise • Logically ordered Prompt words: state, list, describe, tell what or which	• Explaining why it happened the way it did, not what happened • Reasons, motives, and interpretation • Grounded in concrete evidence • Shows thought processes used to arrive at conclusions about the teaching situation Prompt words: how, why, in what ways, explain the rationale	• Consider the successes and weaknesses of the lesson • Make decisions about how you would approach a similar situation in the future • Self-analysis • Retrospective consideration Prompt words: how will it influence future instruction?; what would you do differently?

Provide candidates with the list of questions in Figure 3.17, "Practice with the Three Types of Writing," and have them work together in pairs or small groups to decide whether each question calls for descriptive writing, analytical writing, or reflective writing. Don't forget that some questions span two or three of the types of writing. You may find that candidates disagree on the answer in these cases. This is a healthy debate that will help them to understand what is required by each question.

Ask candidates to think carefully about the questions that are provided for their written commentary. Is this question looking for descriptive, analytical, and/or reflective writing?

Figure 3.17. Practice with the Three Types of Writing

Indicate whether each question calls for **D**escriptive, **A**nalytical, or **R**eflective writing.

____ Why did you do this?

____ How did you do this?

____ How does this work?

____ Describe the process in more detail.

____ How does this information connect to student learning?

____ Why sequence the lessons this way?

____ What suggestions did you make to the student?

____ Why did you choose this student?

____ Why did you give the feedback you did?

____ How do you expect the student to use the feedback to improve?

____ What instructional challenges does the student present?

____ How do these activities build on student interests?

____ How did you decide on the value judgments you made about the student?

____ Why did you feel this way?

____ How did you design instruction to meet the challenges?

____ How did your error analysis influence your teaching?

____ What are your future goals?

____ What worked well?

Reflection	
Group size	Pairs
Relevant strands	G, A
Materials	"Analysis/Assessment/Adjustment" overhead
Timeline	I, II
Credit	Based on contributions from Betsy Sales, NBCT

The requirement to write reflectively for the National Board Process is directly related to all five of the Core Propositions, but especially the fourth Core Proposition:

> **Teachers think systematically about their practice and learn from experience.**

Reflective writing about any subject requires deep, systematic thought—which can be honed through practice. Reflective writing about teaching practice gives clear evidence of three distinct thought and action processes:

ANALYSIS: Why am I teaching what I am teaching? Why am I doing what I am doing?

ASSESSMENT: How do I know that students are learning what I am teaching? How do I know that my activities as a teacher are effective?

ADJUSTMENT: What will I do differently in the future?

Use the enlarged copy of the flowchart in Figure 3.18 to make an overhead. Use it to introduce candidates to this thought process, which is required of reflection. Practice reflection by asking candidates to choose a lesson they taught this week, to briefly describe the lesson to a partner, and then to reflect on the lesson aloud using the questions suggested in this projected overhead.

Figure 3.18

ANALYSIS
Why am I teaching what I am teaching?
Why am I doing what I am doing?

ASSESSMENT
How do I know that students are learning what I am teaching?
How do I know that my activities as a teacher are effective?

ADJUSTMENT
What will I do differently in the future?

Getting Useful Feedback	
Group size	N/A
Relevant strands	G, B, I
Materials	Entry drafts
Timeline	II, III

Many teachers are not accustomed to the volume and style of writing required by the portfolio entries. Candidates will find that it is extremely useful to have other candidates assist them in reviewing their writing to ensure that the evidence they have selected provides clear and consistent evidence of the Standards. Since candidates know the Standards well, they have a great deal they can learn from one another's writing and they are each other's best coaches.

At the same time, outside readers are useful as well, and the sheer volume of work to be reviewed must be taken into consideration; candidates do not want to overburden a few colleagues. One strategy is to have several sets of readers, and another is for candidates to ensure that the feedback they do receive will be useful.

Early in the process candidates should begin to identify people who can serve as effective readers. They will want colleagues who can help them recognize if the content is complete, noneducators who can identify problems of clarity and coherence, and proofreaders who can catch grammar and spelling mistakes (although mechanical errors should not affect scoring because the assessment process is standards-based). But the most important feedback will come from readers who can help candidates identify gaps between the evidence and the Standards. If candidates are going to impose on busy people to take the time to help them, they will want to ensure that their readers are enabled to provide useful feedback. Readers will have to be provided with some context for the writing sample through a cursory introduction to the Standards that are the basis of this work. Therefore, **every writing sample that is shared with readers should be prefaced with a cover sheet**.

The cover sheet will help to focus the reader's attention on what matters most: evidence of the Standards. This does not have to mean additional homework for the candidate. Many resources are at his or her disposal, which can be used for this purpose:

- Use the first page of the entry, the italicized statement of the Standards as they apply to that entry.
- Use the "How Will My Response Be Scored" section of the entry.
- Use the "Scoring Path," which is included in the Scoring Guide.
- Use the "Portfolio Entry Directions" T-chart which the candidate may have created (see Strand C: *Reading and Understanding Directions*).

OR

- Use the "Composing My Written Commentary" from the entry directions, which gives the questions to which the candidate has responded (if they are not already embedded in the writing.)

Candidates should simply photocopy the relevant pages and staple them to the front of each entry draft before asking any of their readers to provide feedback.

Clear, Consistent, and Convincing Evidence	
Group size	**Small groups**
Relevant strands	**G, B**
Materials	**Copies of the writing samples in Figure 3.19**
Timeline	**I, II, III**

In developing their portfolios, candidates are striving to provide "clear, consistent, and convincing evidence" that they meet the Standards. The NBPTS provides everything candidates need to be sure their evidence meets the Standards. There are no secrets; the portfolio entry directions provide a specific articulation of the Standards as they apply to each entry, and the Scoring Guide provides the actual scoring rubrics assessors use. Candidates can use these tools to help them serve as their own assessors and to evaluate the clarity of the evidence they have provided to represent their own teaching.

The writing samples provided in Figure 3.19 were created in an attempt to contrast writing samples that have clear, consistent and convincing evidence with ones that do not provide enough evidence that the Standards have been met. In general, an accomplished response should show clear, consistent, and convincing evidence of:

- Teaching related to worthwhile instructional goals
- Teaching that is appropriate for these students, at this time, in this setting
- A classroom environment that shows evidence of active learning
- Effective teacher reflection
- Command of content

Be sure to check your own Standards and/or Scoring Guide for specific guidance relevant to your certificate.

As candidates compare the writing samples, they should think together about what makes the writing in the left-hand column more clear, consistent, and convincing than the samples on the right. See if you can identify useful patterns, strategies or literary devices.

Candidates can then work together to search for strategies they have used in their own writing: What have we done to make our writing clear? Consistent? Convincing?

By examining, contrasting and discussing writing samples in their candidate support seminars, candidates will learn to articulate their teaching clearly, consistently, and convincingly. This skill will serve these teachers well in their work with student teachers, new teachers, and other new roles.

Figure 3.19. Writing Sample #1A

In this sample, a high school Science teacher describes his efforts to support student inquiry in a videotaped small-group lesson.

Version A

The third segment begins about three minutes into the class wrap-up. We are discussing the data the students have obtained. I explained that I wanted to hear results from whatever groups had completed the component experiment we were discussing but that I wasn't going to analyze one group's results in-depth. My intention was to solicit results for each of the tests and ask the students questions about their significance and ask if they had any questions. I had to keep in mind that this was not the final wrap-up for the investigation, but a check at the halfway point. Most teams had finished the initial analysis of the garden muck soil and would be engaging in the design of the improved soil next time. While I didn't know exact answers to lab tests, I wanted to make sure that the students weren't too far off before they proceeded to next stage.

As the segment begins we are discussing the phosphorus results, having finished the nitrogen results prior to taping. Three students offer results and one, Chrissie, expressed a concern for the accuracy of her results they could be anywhere from 10 to 75 lbs./acre. Another, Nancy, says that her results were in a range. I used this opportunity to discuss the precision of these tests. As tests meant for farming, they are not very precise, but I asked Chrissie to check her results next class. We go on to discuss the potassium results, a nutrient lacking in my "garden muck".

Version B

The third segment begins about three minutes into the class wrap-up. We are discussing what students did. I explained what I wanted. I noticed that the students appear to be talking a great deal. My intention was to ask if they had any questions. I had to keep in mind that this was not the final wrap-up for the investigation. Most teams had finished the initial analysis of the garden muck soil and would be engaging in the design of the improved soil next time. While I didn't know exact answers to lab tests, I wanted to make sure that the students did it right.

As the segment begins we are discussing the phosphorus results, having finished the nitrogen results prior to taping. Three students offer results and one, Chrissie, was confused and kept asking questions about her results, but most of the other kids seemed to get it. They could be anywhere from 10 to 75 lbs./acre. Another, Nancy, says that her results were in a range. I told her for this test the results didn't matter. We go on to discuss the potassium results, a nutrient lacking in my "garden muck".

cont.

Figure 3.19. Writing Sample #1A (cont.)

I asked Tyler (fourth row, left side) to tell us the results of his soil composition test. I had worked with him earlier (after segment two) and knew he was on track to get accurate results. I knew I could also call on Erica, but Tyler is quiet in class and this was his chance to contribute. I recorded his results and used them to anticipate the use of a chart in the book to characterize the soil. If I had more time, I would have done some of that right then. It was interesting that the students made a connection to Tyler's data when discussing the perc test.

In discussing the perc test, I again said that I didn't know the results to encourage the students to find an authoritative answer themselves. They do this during the next class. Since the perc tests aren't fully done, I don't want to discuss actual data and declare it a good result. Next, the conversation takes on a more hypothetical turn. Ben and Chrissie (who weren't involved in their group's perc test) both predicted that the perc would be somewhat between the percs for clay and sand given the soils composition (Tyler's data). We then discuss what to compare the data to. I am trying to ask questions to keep the students engaged in the inquiry. Ben suggested adding sand to increase drainage; Nancy and Rita suggested adding organic matter. There was some disagreement as to organic matter's effect on drainage. Something that will lead to interesting experiments next class. Vicki brought up the effect organic matter will have on fertility, an impact that would be a major focus of the classes in which they begin to alter (improve) the soil. New questions had been developed from the day's work. I was pleased that they were ready to begin the next stage of the lab.

I asked Tyler (fourth row, left side) to tell us the results of his soil composition test, although he usually doesn't participate. I recorded his results and used them to anticipate the use of a chart in the book to characterize the soil. Some students even made a connection to Tyler's data later in the lesson.

In discussing the perc test, I again said that I didn't know the results. I didn't give the results of the perc test because that will be the assignment for the next class. Since the perc tests aren't fully done, I don't want to discuss actual data and declare it a good result. Next, the conversation takes on a more hypothetical turn. Ben and Chrissie (who weren't involved in their group's perc test) both predicted that the perc would be somewhat between the percs for clay and sand given the soils composition (Tyler's data). We then discuss what to compare the data to. I am trying to ask questions to keep the students engaged in the inquiry. Ben suggested adding sand to increase drainage; Nancy and Rita suggested adding organic matter. There was some disagreement as to organic matter's effect. One student brought up some ideas that we might talk about later. They could be a major focus of the classes in which they begin to alter (improve) the soil so I don't want to spoil it. I was pleased that they were right where I wanted them to be by the end of the class: ready for the next stage of the lab.

Figure 3.19. Writing Sample #1B

Writing Sample #1B:

In this sample, a high school Science teacher discusses how a videotaped lesson met his goals.

Version A

It is hard to distill five classes into a twenty-minute videotape. As I watch the whole that I am most satisfied. I think that the design engaged the students in a real-world scenario. There was real interest in designing a better soil, and a significant bit of competition. Although, in another class, the students decided to share information between groups, which was an interesting development. I would say that these students really enjoyed the challenge of this investigation.

I think that I did a reasonably good job of having the students frame the investigation with their own questions. I did this by constantly asking questions myself. I never said that they needed to do X, Y, or Z. Rather, I had them investigate soils and tomatoes and then simply had to ask them what tests they thought were important. Because the amount of content is limited; the students couldn't get too far afield in the factors they identified as important.

Having the students improve the soil was necessary in order to keep this from being simply an exercise in soil analysis technique. While this redesign is not evident on the tape, it is evident in the student letters that I have included as artifacts. You can see that the students needed to take their analysis of the initial soil, hypothesize relevant adjustments, test the improved soil and make further adjustments. While this is not typical "pure" science, given the emphasis in the

Version B

It is hard to distill five classes into a twenty-minute videotape. As I watch the tape, I see a lot that I like. However, it is when I consider the investigation as a whole that I am most satisfied. I think that it's good for students to do real world science. Most kids enjoyed designing a better soil, and there was a significant bit of competition. In another class, the students decided to share information between groups, and this group on the tape didn't. I would say that these students probably enjoyed the challenge of this investigation.

I think that I did a reasonably good job of having the students frame the investigation with their own questions. They did it all on their own; I didn't have to ask them to do anything. Rather, I had them investigate soils and tomatoes and then simply had to ask them what tests they thought were important. The students didn't get too far afield in the factors they identified as important.

I had students improve the soil so it would not only be a simple exercise in soil analysis technique. While this rede-

cont.

Figure 3.19. Writing Sample #1B (cont.)

state frameworks on engineering, design, and technology, it is an appropriate goal. As I watched this tape, I was struck by how well the students could make connections. This is especially evident during the post-lab when the students, discussing perc tests, make connections to the soil composition data provided by Tyler. They also made connections between organic matter as a way to change drainage and its effect on fertility. In this way, the post-lab at this intermediate stage was especially effective in getting the students to continue to frame the investigation. They were in charge of each step.

It was also important that I designed a part of the lab to be a student-designed experiment. I could not expect the students to design procedures for nitrogen analysis or measuring pH. However, they could develop a test for percolation. The procedure would be simple and yet hard enough to do accurately that it would present a challenge. In this part of the class, the students were engaging in true scientific research; they had to determine the controls, variables and ways to make sense of the data. I was happy with the result.

sign is not evident on the tape, it is evident in the student letters that I have included as artifacts. You can see that the students took their analysis of the initial soil, hypothesized relevant adjustments, tested the improved soil and made further adjustments. While this is not typical "pure" science, given the emphasis in the state frameworks on engineering, design, and technology, I think it was a good idea anyway.

As I watched this tape, I saw that the students could make connections— students were talking to each other. The students were discussing perc tests, and making connections to the soil composition data provided by Tyler. They also made connections between organic matter as a way to change drainage and its effect on fertility. The post-lab at this intermediate stage helped the students to continue to frame the investigation because I made them do each step.

It was also important that a part of the lab involved a student-designed experiment. I knew that they could develop a test for percolation. The procedure would be simple. In this part of the class, the students were engaging in true scientific research, just like real scientists, with real goggles and all. I was happy with the result.

Figure 3.19. Writing Sample #2

In this sample, a Middle Childhood Generalist teacher discusses changes she might make in her teaching choices as a result of reflecting on the video.

Writing Sample #2:

Version A

The structure of my classroom meetings has been influenced primarily by the writings of Jane Nelsen (Positive Discipline and Positive Discipline in the Classroom) and H. Stephen Glenn (Developing Capable People). I view the meetings as opportunities to develop capable students who have a responsibility for the smooth operation of the classroom and the school. In these sessions students' ideas are taken seriously to build confidence, courage, and self-esteem.

In the videotape of the first group, in which Johnny mentions the boys call him "Chunky," I am disappointed that I was too quick to say, "So it doesn't bother you." When in fact, it obviously did bother Johnny. I am disappointed that I missed the expression on his face, which told something different than his words. I have since taken the time to discuss this further with him. When a difficult situation arises, he will now try to remember to use an "I" message with his peers such as when they call him that name. I have taught him how to seek out peer support, so that by discussing the situation further with Gene and Danny who live in his neighborhood, he can help himself when he has trouble with the other boys. This support has helped to build Johnny's self-confidence.

The preceding example shows that I still need to work on listening to students' comments and allowing them plenty of time to speak. I also need to focus on asking students to explain further when an issue such as Johnny's comes up, so that the student can be empowered to deal with the issue and feel capable.

In reviewing this tape, I realize that Lori in the first group quietly said, "After the

Version B

Our fifth grade has scheduled classroom meetings. The structure of my classroom meetings has been influenced primarily by some of the readings I did in college. According to these books the meetings are opportunities to develop capable students who have a responsibility for the smooth operation of the classroom and the school. Through these meetings I expect the students to build social skills.

In the videotape of the first group, in which Johnny mentions the boys call him "Chunky," I wish they didn't call him that. It disappointed me even though it didn't bother Johnny. I am disappointed that I missed the expression on his face, which told something different than his words. Maybe that's why he made that face on the video. I didn't have time to talk with him about it. When a difficult situation arises, he is trying to remember to use an "I" message with his peers when they call him that name. I told him that he should rely on Gene and Danny, who live in the same neighborhood, to help him when he has trouble with the other boys.

The preceding example shows that I still need to work on keep-

cont.

Figure 3.19. Writing Sample #2 (cont.)

bell rings…" as a next issue to discuss, but no one heard her. I must remember to encourage students to discuss all the issues before moving on, and I need to encourage students to speak up and to help students develop ways to be heard so that their ideas can be explored. I also need to address ways to handle occasions when a student's suggestion is not discussed. In my teaching, I try to emphasize and model that each student has a valuable contribution to make to the discussions.

Another opportunity I missed was to explore with the second group why the fifth grade girls interfere with the boys playing football, what this action communicates, and ways to solve it. The girls are probably doing this because they feel they need attention from the boys; I need to help them find constructive ways to get positive attention. This is an important agenda issue which we will need to take up at another class meeting.

In the first group, I wish I had explored with the students why they think the fourth graders behave as they described. This would have then given the students an opportunity to consider difficulties the fourth graders may be experiencing and then we could have looked at possible solutions.

This self-examination was perhaps one of the most difficult tasks I have ever accomplished. I am concerned about the number of missed opportunities that I could have asked students to clarify and explore more deeply. Obviously there is room for improvement; so I have made a list to remind me of areas of focus for future class meetings, and I will explore these with my students. I am passionate in my role of empowering students to build successful classroom communities because it is here that students have an opportunity to discover, learn, and practice the skills that lead to a meaningful and productive life: listening, responsibility, cooperation, problem-solving, conflict-resolution, self-discipline, mutual respect, communication, and accountability.

ing students to a time limit so that they will all have time to speak. Maybe in my next meeting we can find a way to work on this issue.

In reviewing this tape, I realize that Lori in the first group quietly said, "After the bell rings…" as a next issue to discuss, but no one heard her. Lori never speaks loudly enough, so of course no one heard her. I need to work on listening harder. I also need to address ways to handle occasions when a student's suggestion is not discussed. In my teaching, I try to make sure everyone gets a chance to speak.

Another opportunity I missed was to explore with the second group why the fifth grade girls interfere with the boys playing football, what this action communicates, and ways to solve it. If I had the time I would take this up at another class meeting.

In the first group, I wish I had explored with the students why they think the fourth graders behave as they described. This way I could have provided possible solutions. When I worked in another school, there was a similar issue; we didn't let them get away with this. There was away to deal with it.

As a result of this self-examination I know what I will do differently next time to help make sure my students have the skills they will need when they grow up.

Strand H

Assessment Center Preparation

Preparing for the content knowledge assessment is a great opportunity for candidates to expand their knowledge beyond the scope of the units they are accustomed to teaching, to review the full range of material that is appropriate for a given developmental level, and perhaps even to think about new ways to approach old material. It piques teachers' curiosity about what others in their field are teach- ing and how they are teaching it, and leads many of them to new ideas and resources. Many find it empowering to have their com- mand of their content chal- lenged and acknowledged. Others recognize glaring gaps in their knowledge and they gain new direction and motivation for their learning.

The assessment will include six 30-minute exercises designed to assess the depth and breadth of candidates' content knowledge. Candidates working in groups have a number of ways that they can work together to challenge and improve their content knowledge, in preparation for this assessment exercise.

Following are strategies that candidate groups have used to support one another in preparing for the assessment center portion of the certification process.

Assessment Center Interface	
Group size	Individual
Relevant strands	H
Materials	Computer with Internet access
Timeline	IV

After spending hundreds of hours in front of a computer creating portfolio entries, it may be difficult to imagine that candidates need to spend more time practicing computer skills. However, the unfamiliar environment, the timed setting, and the natural anxiety that candidates feel can make the computer-based assessment difficult for many people. In addition, increasing numbers of candidates are choosing to complete the assessment center exercise before or during their portfolio development. Practice with the NBPTS assessment center interface can help to make the experience easier for candidates, allowing them to focus their attention on providing evidence of their content knowledge.

The NBPTS Web site has a Candidate Resource Center. The online tutorial provided through this page of the National Board's Web site is useful in familiarizing candidates with the look and feel of the testing environment. Although the tutorial does allow candidates to practice a timed response, it does not include content-specific questions for each certificate area. As the current assessment center prompts are retired, they are likely to become available to candidates through the National Board's Web site as well.

Study Groups	
Group size	Certificate-specific groups
Relevant strands	H, B
Materials	Certificate Overviews, State/National Curriculum Standards, trade books, etc.
Timeline	IV

Candidates are, again, one another's best resources. As they discover gaps in their content knowledge, they should work in certificate groups to brainstorm a bibliography of resources that will be useful to study. Candidates will benefit from sharing their own knowledge as well as the resources they can access through their schools.

Many teachers are familiar with the one or two math programs used in their schools; one group I worked with brainstormed a list of several popular math programs with which they thought they should all be familiar. They arranged to bring materials from each of these math programs to the group and worked together to compare and contrast the pedagogical differences between the math programs.

State and national content standards documents are useful study tools (see Appendix D). Candidates can use these documents to create a list of the many different topics that are considered appropriate for a given developmental level. Candidates should also check their school libraries or teacher resource centers for curriculum guides, scope and sequence charts, and trade books. These resources help teachers identify what other teachers at their same grade level are teaching and how. They call candidates to account by asking probing questions: There are many subjects being taught at your grade level and many different ways to teach these subjects. What is your rationale for teaching the content you are teaching, the way you are teaching it, to the students you have, at this time, in this setting?

As candidates prepare together for the assessment center exercise, they might challenge each other to think about how they would provide evidence of the kind of thinking that underlies accomplished teaching and appropriate rationales for their choices.

☞   **Note**: If your candidate group creates a bibliography, be sure to keep a copy to share with next year's candidates!

Study Planning	
Group size	Certificate-specific groups
Relevant strands	H
Materials	Certificate Overviews
Timeline	IV

Candidates should use the "Certificate Overviews," which are provided on the NBPTS Web site to identify the topics that will be addressed in their six assessment center exercises. Note that some certificate areas have room for an element of choice (for example, Exceptional Needs candidates can choose a developmental level), but others do not. Yet, inevitably, teachers find that some of the content areas to be assessed are outside of what they regularly teach. High school physics teachers may have to demonstrate competency in chemistry, early childhood generalists who teach life science to second graders may have to discuss a kindergarten unit on magnets, and sixth-grade math teachers may have to know about eighth-grade algebra. This is a chance for candidates to round out their knowledge, to expand their focus, and maybe even make new content connections that will enrich their teaching.

Once candidates have a clear idea of the scope of the content to be assessed, they should assess what they know and what they need to know. A simple organizer such as the one in Figure 3.20 can help candidates be more strategic about identifying gaps in their knowledge. Teachers who spend time in honest reflection of the gaps in their practice will have clear direction about professional learning goals; they will know exactly what they need to work on to become accomplished teachers.

Figure 3.20

Sample study plan for the Early Childhood/Generalist certificate

I: Literacy		II: Mathematics		III: Science		IV: Social Studies		V: Children's Play		VI: PE, Health and Safety	

List all possible subtopics in left column.

Use the right column to list resources that can help you master the content or to check off the topic if/when you have mastered it.

Strand I

Continuing Candidates

The National Board Certification process is a rigorous one that requires teachers to provide clear, consistent, and convincing evidence. Almost half of the candidates who pursue certification find that it takes more than 1 year to achieve certification. Candidates may send in as many entries as they are able to complete, bank the passing scores that they receive, then retake any entries they have not completed or which have received a score of less than 2.75.[4] They then have two more years to complete their candidacy. If candidates are thinking of National Board Certification as a professional growth experience and not a test, they will continue to pursue it until they grow to become accomplished teachers. Many "test takers" think the game is over when they do not achieve on the first try.

Following is a list of activities given in this "Toolkit" that may be especially useful in working with candidates who are continuing their candidacy beyond the first year. Your candidates have special needs at this time and in this setting. Determine what their needs are, using activities from Strand A and use that information to make decisions about which other activities will be appropriate.

 Note: Don't forget that continuing candidates have expertise they can share with other candidates in the areas in which they have received accomplished scores.

From Strand A

- These Candidates, at This Time, in This Setting

If you are working with continuing candidates with whom you did not work the first time around, be sure to use this activity. You need to know with whom you are working and what they need from you, but, more importantly, *they* need to think about what they need.

- Fears Activity

You need to know what these candidates are most concerned about, and you need for them to know the boundaries of how you can help them and how you cannot. If they are aware of their own fears, they can confront their fears more effectively.

From Strand B

- Seeing Yourself in the Standards

Encourage candidates to obtain a new, unmarked copy of the Standards. As they go through the process of highlighting and making margin notes, encourage them to reflect on changes they have made in their practice as a result of their first year of candidacy.

- Internalizing the Standards

Candidates are certified when they are able to present evidence that they can practice at the level of the Standards. Continuing candidates would do well to use these given strategies to be certain that they understand and have internalized the Standards.

- Vocabulary of Accomplished Practice

Reviewing the vocabulary of accomplished practice can help continuing candidates in two important ways. It can help them to be sure that they understand and have internalized the Standards; most of these terms come directly from the Standards documents. It can also help candidates who see the writing task of this assessment as a barrier to certification. This list helps put useful words into their lexicon so that they can concisely and accurately describe the learning and teaching in their classrooms.

- Examining the Rubric

After creating a new T-chart of accomplished/not accomplished practice, assist candidates to use the chart to examine their own scored entries. When they use the chart to examine their entries together with others, they will benefit from the pressure to be honest and open-minded.

From Strand C

• Reading and Understanding Directions

This may help candidates to have a clearer understanding of the task, so that they can determine whether a low score was caused by misreading the directions or by misunderstanding what was valued.

• Curriculum Mapping

Continuing candidates will find curriculum mapping a useful tool as they lay out the year's work and strategically schedule ample opportunities to rework portfolio entries.

From Strand D

• Making Good Choices

Candidates who did not receive a passing score on the Documented Accomplishments entry should use this activity to help them reflect on the effectiveness of the choices they made before making new choices. Candidates can use the same accomplishments if they decide this is the best choice (since accomplishments can be from the past 5 years), but the written commentary must be wholly new.

• Sample Accomplishments

When candidates need to rework a Documented Accomplishments entry, they often want to or need to use the same accomplishments. The challenge is in determining how to rework the writing in a more effective way. This exercise may reveal for candidates that there are many ways to analyze and reflect on an accomplishment.

From Strand E

• Choosing Student Work Samples

This activity may help candidates make thoughtful choices as they select work samples that reveal the architecture of accomplished teaching underlying their practice.

From Strand F

• Tape Critique

See if candidates are willing to share their own scored tapes. Continuing candidates who have accomplished video entries will appreciate the opportunity to share their expertise; videos that received lower scores are rich sources of learning too.

From Strand G

- Distinguishing between the Three Types of Writing

Candidates should carefully review the questions given for each written commentary and decide what kind of writing is required. Ask candidates to review their own scored entries and highlight and/or demarcate the passages that are descriptive, analytical, and/or reflective. Did they provide the type of writing that the prompt required?

- Getting Useful Feedback

The suggestions in this activity are especially important if candidates are planning to use some of the same readers.

From Strand H

- Study Planning

Candidates are already familiar with the interface, and they do not have their scored entries to review. The only productive preparation in which they can engage is making sure that they have confidence and comprehensive knowledge in their content. Candidates who plan to retake the assessment center exercise should take the time to strategically identify the gaps in their knowledge and create a plan for mastering that knowledge.

- Study Groups

Candidates should take advantage of the resources in Appendix D to create their own study questions, and they should work together to share knowledge and resources.

Notes

1   Saphier, J., & M. King (1985). Good seeds grow in strong cultures. Educational Leadership. (42), 67-73.

2   The "Architecture of Accomplished Teaching" is not a trademark of NBPTS, but is used in NBPTS Facilitators' Institutes to illustrate the importance of teacher focus on "these students, at this time, in this setting." www.nbpts.org

3.   Jacobs, Heidi Hayes (1997). "Integrating the Curriculum." Paper presented at the Cambridge Public Schools, Cambridge, MA.

4   Candidates should be aware that there is a fee for retakes.

4. Improving the Culture of Teaching

A Guide to Life after Candidacy

You put your blood, sweat, tears, and a whole lot more into a cardboard carton smaller than a breadbox. You look over your list, check it twice, then head off to the post office. You stand in line, clutching the box to your chest until it is time to hand it over to an unknowing postal worker, a perfect stranger who asks you if you want a receipt. The look on your face tells her, "of course," although a carbon copy of illegible scrawl on a triplicate form hardly seems a fair trade for what you've given her. She tosses your precious box into a bin with other "important" packages: returns from mail-order catalogues, contracts that need immediate signatures, and birthday presents from Grandma. "Next!?" she calls out, before you are ready. It echoes in your head... it is a good question.

It is impossible to describe the surging sense of agency that many candidates feel after completing the process of National Board Certification. They thought they had just finished a marathon, but they realize on the way home from the post office that they only just finished training for it. They swore that they never wanted to see another videotaped lesson again, but they continue taping lessons and analyzing them with colleagues.

111

They vowed that they would never look back at the writing they worked and reworked for their portfolios; now they peek into those files with thoughts of publishing and presenting the work. They sigh with relief that they will now have more time in their lives for family and leisure. Then they start a new induction program for the district, write a grant to support increased professional development, join the superintendent's advisory committee, begin presenting at regional and national conferences, become president of the local union, or design a seminar to support new candidates for National Board Certification. A National Board study tried to quantify this impulse in a survey of the impact of National Board Certification on teachers. (See Figure 4.1.) Of the NBCTs surveyed, 74 percent reported that they had taken on new professional roles within their school, district, or community.[1] Future research may be able to tell us more about the specific knowledge and skills that have been nurtured in these teachers through the process, and about the kinds of roles for which NBCTs are uniquely prepared. But in the meantime, NBCTs are not waiting. They are taking on existing roles, creating new roles themselves, and they are stepping into roles selectively chosen for them by others.

Figure 4.1. New Professional Roles and Activities

In 2001 NBPTS conducted two surveys of nearly 500 NBCTs and assessors to examine the impact of National Board Certification on these teachers.

74% of survey respondents said achieving National Board Certification had affected their roles and activities *within* their school, district, or community.

The most frequent new professional roles and activities were:

• Serving on committees in school, district, community, or union (37%)

• Mentoring NBCT candidates or advocating for NBPTS (37%)

• Mentoring, advising, or sharing ideas with colleagues (33%)

About half of respondents said being an NBCT has affected their roles and activities *outside* their school district.

The most frequent new professional roles and activities were:

• Mentoring NBCT candidates or advocating for NBPTS (37%)

• Serving on regional, state, or national education-related committees (31%)

• Increasing interaction with colleagues, including presenting at conferences and workshops (31%)

Reprinted with permission from the National Board for Professional Teaching Standards, www.nbpts.org/research/archive. All rights reserved.

Connecting NBCTs to new professional roles is the key to using National Board Certification to improve the culture of teaching, but it is easier said than done. Some NBCTs build up resentment and frustration while waiting for administrators to recognize them for new roles. Others want to seek out new roles on their own but are hindered by practical, financial, or political barriers. Lack of specialized training or confidence may also inhibit NBCTs from taking on the roles they really do desire. Since National Board Certified Teachers are well trained in understanding teaching and learning and since they are well placed close to where teaching and learning happens in schools throughout the country, they have the capacity that other education reforms need to succeed. Administrators, policy makers, and researchers must support work to connect these teachers to new roles that will capitalize on their expertise. This section provides practical strategies for connecting NBCTs to new professional roles.

Figure 4.2

Improving the Culture of Teaching Through New Roles

NBCTs can take on existing roles	NBCTs can seek out or create new roles for themselves	NBCTs can be asked to take on new roles
• Mentoring • Content-area and curriculum consulting • School governance • Union leadership	• Professional development leaders • Researchers • Higher education partners • Administrators	• Advisors • Panel experts • Local leaders • Research partners

NBCTs can take on existing roles

There are a number of existing roles into which NBCTs can step immediately. These roles are already established in most places and are routinely taken on by willing volunteers; NBCTs who rise to the occasion may have something unique to offer.

Mentoring. Mentoring is one of the most common professional activities of NBCTs. It is not a new role for most, but the process of portfolio development is likely to have helped these teachers develop an increased facility for articulating the complicated processes of teaching and learning. Their increased sense of capacity makes them all the more eager to share their knowledge and skill with others. Their experience with using data to identify needs and reflecting on their practice to inform next steps can be tremendously valuable in their work with new and student teachers. Their intimate knowledge of the National Board Certification process will enable them to serve as effective mentors for future NBCT candidates.

A note to NBCTs who want to begin mentoring . . .

NBCTs can pursue mentoring activities in a variety of ways. Many schools and districts already have programs in place, which coordinate the match-up between mentors and mentees. If your school or district does not have such a program, you certainly could start one, but you also have other options. To work with student teachers, you can contact teacher preparation programs at local colleges and universities directly and ask them if they are in need of mentors or "cooperating practitioners." You should do this in the semester before you would like to begin. For this work you will typically receive a voucher to take a free course and/or a stipend. To work with new teachers, you might just extend yourself to the new teachers in your own school. You can always work through the director of personnel to identify new teachers in the district and often teachers' unions will make resources available for this work. Unless you connect with an existing program or start one yourself, you are unlikely to be compensated for this work. To work with candidates for National Board Certification, you can contact the regional NBPTS representative (identified on the NBPTS Web site) to find out how candidate support is coordinated in your area. In some areas it is facilitated through colleges or the state department of education; in others it is done directly through local districts or unions; in still other areas, there is no coordination at all. Coordinated programs often carry a stipend or salary that is funded through grants or course fees. You should contact your regional representative through the NBPTS Web site to start.

Content-area and curriculum specialists. National Board Certified Teachers have demonstrated that they know their content and know how to teach that content to their students. The assessment center exercises testify to their mastery of content knowledge; the portfolio provides evidence that they can effectively use their content knowledge together with their knowledge of students to create meaningful learning experiences for their students. They are therefore well suited to take on a variety of professional roles in which content-area and curriculum expertise is needed. NBCTs have the knowledge and skills to develop district curriculum and professional development plans, to serve as department leaders in their schools, and to join standards-drafting committees.They may also use their expertise to make important contributions in professional associations.

A note to NBCTs who want to serve as content-area and curriculum consultants...

To begin working in these areas, you will need to make connections with key school leaders and professional associations, and you should not be shy about your accomplishments. It will also be helpful if you are adept at using the Internet as many content-area and curriculum opportunities are posted on the Web. To pursue roles in developing curriculum for your district, for example, you will need to be familiar with the district's plans and priorities. You can then offer services aligned with these plans and ask to be written into future grants so that you will be compensated. You should also find out what the district is spending on professional development and who is under contract to provide it. Why shouldn't it be you?

The way that leadership positions within a content area (such as English department head, or Math team chair) are filled varies from site to site. In some cases these are volunteer positions, which are passed from teacher to teacher like a hot potato, and in others they are stipended positions that are filled on the basis of seniority. In all cases, they hold the potential to be important vantage points for improving the quality of teaching and learning. NBCTs who want to make a difference should seek to serve in these roles.

Participating in standards-drafting committees and review panels is a good way to build new connections with practitioners from other school settings. Professional associations are always looking for nominations of teachers to participate, and you can usually nominate yourself. You should make it a habit to browse the Web sites of professional associations that are relevant to your interests, (see Appendix D) as well as those of other agencies such as your state's department of education. These advisory roles are usually unpaid, although there is often reimbursement for expenses.

School governance roles. Today there are increasing opportunities for teachers to participate in school governance as education reforms are encouraging various forms of site-based and distributed leadership. What National Board Certified Teachers can bring to the table is a disciplined focus on teaching and learning. It is easy for a school-site council, an administrative leadership team, a local school committee, or even the state board of education to lose sight of the ultimate goal of the whole enterprise: improved teaching and increased levels of learning. Sometimes it takes an accomplished teacher who can bring an articulate perspective from the daily life of the classroom to make positive changes.

A note to NBCTs who want to take on roles in school governance...

To become an active participant in school governance, you will usually have to be elected or make yourself known as someone who wants to be appointed. In either case you will have to campaign with a clearly articulated position about teaching and learning, which is no problem for an NBCT.

Union leaders. The National Board Certification process may not necessarily groom teachers in the skills needed to be effective union leaders. But NBCTs who do become union leaders are in a tremendous position to ensure that National Board Certification is being used to improve the quality of teaching practice and teaching culture in their district. Whether they become part of the union leadership, or work through its committees, NBCTs can position themselves to make sure the membership is educated about National Board Certification, candidates are supported to work in groups throughout their candidacy year, new roles are created that tap the capacity of NBCTs, and NBCTs are compensated for their new roles through contract language.

A note to NBCTs who want to take on roles as union leaders . . .

Becoming an elected building representative in your local union is not the only way to get involved in union work. Most local and state union affiliates have numerous opportunities to serve on committees that have influence on the culture of teaching. They recommend policy, bargain contract language, educate membership and the public about key issues, support and provide professional development, and represent teachers in dealings with school administration. Contact your local or state affiliate to learn about these opportunities, or contact your national affiliate—the National Education Association or the American Federation of Teachers, both founding constituents of NBPTS—to learn more about how you can get involved on the national level.

NBCTs can seek out new roles for themselves

While some NBCTs are taking on familiar roles in and around the school community, other NBCTs prefer to seek out new roles for themselves. We know that NBCTs are adept at using evidence to identify needs; some of these teachers want to start new programs to address those needs. We also know that NBCTs have worked on making their tacit knowledge explicit; some of these teachers want to seek out new opportunities to contribute to the knowledge base in the profession. These teachers may have to go beyond the skills they have honed in the National Board process. They will have to be persuasive and resourceful. They will have to be able to convince others of the need for these new roles, to persuade others that they are the ones to take this work on, to rally support for their ideas, and to write grants and garner the resources necessary to bring their initiatives to fruition. Many NBCTs are doing just that.

Professional development leaders. Entrepreneurial NBCTs are taking bold steps to become leaders in professional development. They attend conferences as presenters and active participants; they offer in-service workshops in their districts and throughout the region; and they publish articles that stimulate professional discourse on topics that are central to improved teaching and learning.

A note to NBCTs who want to become professional development leaders . . .

To take part in professional conferences, join the professional associations that are in your field. You will be invited to participate in meetings, to make conference presentations, and to submit articles to their journals. Many national associations have state or regional affiliations that make frequent participation much more feasible.

Before you begin marketing yourself as a professional development provider, you will first want to have some conference presentations under your belt. Decide which one or two topics you want to develop from your repertoire and submit conference proposals on these topics. This is a great way to practice your presentation while building a list of references for your resume. Next offer your services within your district; try different settings and formats to see what works best. Once you have perfected your instructional plan, you can approach other districts in the region and ask anywhere from $20 to $100 per hour for your services (depending on the size of the group and other factors).

Many NBCTs have the impulse to develop some of their portfolio writing into pieces for publication. They have already analyzed and reflected on their practices and handcrafted a carefully worded essay about them. But strong professional communities are characterized by open and informed dialogue. It is important for us to listen as well as speak. Before you enter the conversation, you will need to know what people have been talking about. Eavesdrop on the conversation awhile by subscribing to relevant journals. You can often read the current edition of educational journals and periodicals for free on the Internet. When you are ready to add your two cents, make sure that your work addresses the critical issues in the field.

Researchers. The certification process is really a structured inquiry process for researching one's own practice. Many teachers find that it whets their appetite and they want to pursue further research. They might initiate action research projects at their own school sites or forge collaborations with research institutions that are looking for teacher-researchers to bring the wisdom of practice to their studies. In either case, they are combining their new grounded knowledge about the power of data with their desire to address important questions about teaching and learning.

A note to NBCTs who want to become involved in research . . .

To initiate action research projects within your school, you can simply work with colleagues to identify research questions and apply a structured inquiry process (much like the National Board process) that will lead to new informed actions. It is empowering, it builds collegiality, it generates solutions that cater to their own unique setting, and it will lead to improved student learning.[2] No special resources are necessary to engage in action research—just find a partner and begin. Or use one of the many professional guides that are available to help you structure your inquiry.[3] When you are ready to share your findings in professional journals or periodicals, be sure to take time to learn about the conventions that govern educational research. Most publications provide guidelines for submissions that you will need to follow. Connecting to research projects and research institutions is a bit harder. Educational research is not yet strategically coordinated enough for teachers to learn about studies before they begin. Researchers tend to reach out to the teachers they know or through schools they have already worked with. To break into the network of university-based research projects, you might approach a target institution and offer to provide an informational session about the work of the National Board for Professional Teaching Standards or some other area of relevant expertise. You might also simply present them with a letter of introduction. Some institutions have Web sites that list ongoing projects; while it may be too late to join these projects in progress, you will begin to learn which researchers are working on topics that align with your own interests and you can make contact with them.

Higher education partners. Institutions of higher education have a variety of exciting roles that are appropriate for National Board Certified Teachers. These positions usually require a bit more initiative on the part of the teacher to go out and find them. From taking on adjunct faculty positions, to redesigning or working with teacher preparation programs, to serving as a consultant for accreditation visits, these positions not only offer an opportunity to connect with professionals from outside their school community, but they can offer a real opportunity for career advancement. The work that NBCTs have done to collect and reflect on evidence of their teaching comes in handy here. They have done most of the ground work needed to be able to feel ownership of their field, to be able to guide student teachers to improve their practice in their placements, and to be able to make presentations in an area of expertise.

A note to NBCTs who want to become higher education partners . . .

NBCTs who are interested in working with institutions of higher education might begin by contacting local colleges of education about making informational presentations about National Board Certification. Start with your alma mater's alumni office or the institutions that have sent you student teachers or other colleges with whom you may have connections.[4] This will help you to learn more about how the school is organized and which departments or offices you are interested in working with. Some institutions offer education courses through an education department, others list them under social services, and still others make them available through a continuing education department. The institution may also have a Web site that will help you understand how it is organized. You will need to get to know the dean of the right department if you want to offer your services. To work with teacher preparation programs as a supervisor for students in their placements, simply contact the placement office. This work is only available to teachers who do not have a full-time classroom placement, as you will need to be available to visit your student teachers in their placements during the school day. To work as an adjunct faculty member to teach an existing course, to propose your own course, or to serve as a visiting practitioner for another course, begin by browsing the existing course catalogue (usually available online) to see what you can offer. You will need to prepare a proposal that makes clear to them why they need you, and you will submit it with your resume. Some NBCTs have been able to forge roles for themselves as consultants to help teacher preparation programs prepare for accreditation or licensing regulations. Regardless of whether these programs are seeking NCATE accreditation (which is aligned to the National Board Core Propositions) or state licensing, they will benefit from NBCTs who know well the challenges of collecting evidence to demonstrate a standard.

Administrators. Finally, teachers who have become certified sometimes feel it is time to move into roles in administration. They often see this as another way to make an impact beyond their own classrooms. Their understanding of keen accomplished teaching is likely to make them effective instructional leaders; however, there are other elements of administration that these teachers will have to develop (such as fiscal management skills and knowledge of educational law).

A note to NBCTs who want to take on administrative roles . . .
Teachers who are interested in taking on such roles will have to contact their state agency or department of education to find out about certification requirements. While some of you may choose to enter a preparatory track to become principals, others of you may pioneer new ways to lead without leaving the classroom. You may be able to take on instructional leadership or other administrative duties by working in your classrooms part-time. You can build a persuasive argument for experimenting with these models by using your astute observations of school data to articulate why these nontraditional changes might be necessary.

NBCTs can be asked to take on roles

The most influential roles that NBCTs can take on to improve the culture of teaching are not yet within our own grasp. NBCTs must rely on influential policy makers and administrators to recognize them for these roles. While these teachers sit idly by, educational policy is often made without accomplished voices from the classroom. Research is being conducted without the wisdom of practice. And curriculum is being developed without the expertise of those who understand what underlies good teaching. If politicians and policy makers were to get the right idea to ask a teacher, whom would they ask? There are 3 million teachers in America. How do they choose? The stakes are too high to rely on patronage. NBPTS has been identifying accomplished, reflective teachers for nearly a decade.

Yet there are still many administrators, legislators, and research institutions that do not recognize the capacity that NBCTs can bring to new roles. Following is a list of the types of roles that NBCTs must be asked to take on to capitalize on National Board Certified Teachers in improving the culture of teaching.

Advisory work. National Board Certified Teachers need to be on every state Board of Education. The purpose of these state agencies is to guarantee that every child will have access to a quality education; they cannot carry this out effectively or realistically without an accomplished voice from the classroom. The advisory boards these state agencies convene would likewise benefit from this corps of teachers. NBCTs should be on the boards of professional associations and other agencies that are working to improve or reform education; they can bring the complexities of the school site to the table. Academic and professional journals as well as other publishers of educational materials need these teachers on their review boards so that the good work that is published will explicitly address the pervasive problems of practice and will consistently consider the impact on student learning.

Panel work. Panels are extremely useful structures for getting the perspective of various stakeholders at once. They are used in all professions at conferences and institutes to explore complex issues, and they are used for evaluation or review of programs. The practitioner's perspective is critical on panels that aim to serve the field of education, but it is often glaringly absent. NBCTs are ready to step up to the plate.

Local leadership. Many local opportunities to be a part of reform efforts are appointed positions. Teachers may be appointed to be a department head or director of instruction, to help draft grant proposals and professional development plans, or to represent the school and/or district at conferences. Districts can choose anybody; they should choose someone with the capacity to make a strong impact on teaching and learning— an NBCT.

Research Partnerships. Much of the literature on educational research laments the disconnect between research and practice. Researchers have been able to cite some of the causes for this disconnect: vastly different work settings and cultures, the fact that historically researchers have been men and teachers have been women, and the lack of the presence of research in teacher preparation and therefore in teachers' work lives.[5] The work that NBCTs have done to become articulate about their practice and the experiences they have had with inquiry stand to bring these two communities together in effective and balanced research partnerships. Researchers need to seek them out.

The names and school districts of over 23,000 National Board Certified Teachers are listed on the Web site of the National Board for Professional Teaching Standards. They are currently teaching in all 50 states. Articles by and about National Board Certified Teachers appear in newspapers, professional periodicals, and academic journals regularly. They are not so hard to find, and they are not going away. They are working together as a profession should to improve the quality of teaching for all children.

Notes

1. National Board for Professional Teaching Standards, "The Impact of National Board Certification on Teachers: A Survey of National Board Certified Teachers and Assessors," (Arlington, VA: National Board for Professional Teaching Standards, 2001).

2. Richard Sagor, *Guiding School Improvement with Action Research* (Alexandria, VA: Association for Supervision and Curriculum Development, 2000).

3. Two recommendations are *Action Research: An Educational Leader's Guide to School Improvement* by Jeffrey Glanz (Christopher-Gordon Publishers, Inc., 1998) or *Guiding School Improvement with Action Research* by Richard Sagor (ASCD, 2000).

4. The National Board's Speakers Bureau can provide you with posters, brochures, and even a PowerPoint presentation to assist you in your work as an advocate for the National Board.

5. Richard J. Shavelson and Lisa Towne, eds., *Scientific Research in Education, Committee on Scientific Principles in Education* (Washington D.C.: National Academy Press, 2002).

Appendix A

The Impact of National Board Certification on Teaching Culture and Teachers' Practice: A Summary of the Evidence

While we await convincing empirical evidence that will make a conclusive statement about the impact of National Board Certification on student learning and teaching culture, many stakeholders are relying on preliminary studies and convincing testimonials. A survey of completed research studies is presented here together with a sampling of testimonials. Visit www.nbpts.org for a complete description of current and ongoing research.

On improving the culture of teaching...

Publication	Report title	Relevant findings	Sample
Fall 2001	The Impact of National Board Certification on Teachers: A Survey of NBCTs and Assessors An NBPTS survey conducted by Education Resources Group	• NBCTs report they have received increased recognition and respect, and they are more often sought out for their ideas and opinions	235 NBCTs who achieved certification between 1994-1999 and 236 assessors (75 of whom were NBCTs and 181 non-NBCTs)
Spring 2002	Status of NBCTs in Indiana A study conducted by the Indiana Professional Standards Board	• NBCTs have been offered leadership roles within their schools/districts (62.5%), invited speakers (19%), and members of Disney American Teacher review committees (16%).	32 Indiana NBCTs
November 2001	"I Am a Better Teacher: What Candidates for National Board Certification Say About the Assessment Process" A survey conducted by NBPTS	• Participation in the National Board Certification Process enhances teacher interactions with students (82%), parents and guardians (82%), and helps to improve collaborations with colleagues (81%).	5641 first-time NBCT candidates in the 2000-2001 cycle (after completion but before notification)

Testimonials:

- Nancy Grasmick, Maryland's chief state school officer and secretary-treasurer of the State Board of Education, says, "Maryland has instituted a variety of incentives designed to point more of our best students towards the teaching career path. Once those teachers start their careers, we want them to stay and grow. National Board Certification is part of that. It spotlights the teaching profession, and places proven teachers on a pedestal alongside our other critical professions—exactly where it should be." And in regard to veteran teachers, she says, "It is the best way I've found yet to reengage teachers in this wonderful profession, and—ultimately—to make schools better for our students."

- Robert T. Jones, President and CEO of the National Alliance of Business says, "It is extremely important for teachers to see in front of them career ladders and opportunities to enhance their profession. The most widely respected and supported example of that is National Board Certification because it ensures a quality standard of recognition."

- Wayne McDevitt, member of the North Carolina State Board of Education and vice chancellor for Administration and Financial Affairs at the University of North Carolina at Asheville, says regarding teacher retention, "I continually meet experienced teachers who say they were thinking about leaving the classroom... they were saying, 'I'm either going to go one way or the other.' Then they heard about National Board Certification and they went through the process. It gave them a shot of adrenaline and kept them in teaching at a critical time in their careers."

- Susan Brownlee, executive director of the Grable Foundation (which has awarded a $300,000 grant to increase the number of NBCTs in Pittsburgh), says, "We are pleased to support an organization devoted to building the teaching profession and keeping top-notch teachers in the classroom."

- John Deasy, superintendent of the Santa Monica-Malibu Unified School District and former superintendent of schools in Coventry, Rhode Island, has seen it make a difference. "This is a nationally benchmarked standard of excellence in teaching. It has changed the culture of teaching more than anything else."

- The *St. Louis Post-Dispatch* writes: "Without enough qualified teachers, how will the nation get the accountants, engineers, attorneys and other highly valued professionals it needs? One way is to pay more to teachers who earn certificates from NBPTS. This voluntary program requires teachers to show a higher level of professionalism and has been compared to accountants earning CPAs or attorneys passing bar exams."

- Roberta Doering, a former president of the National School Boards Association and a member of the Agawam, Massachusetts, school committee, says, "One of the best things a school district can do to attract and retain excellent teachers is to support National Board Certification."

- David Coley, principal, Cary High School, says, "I have observed that the process also encourages collegiality across the staff... I have seen this process create bonds between teachers across departments and disciplines. These relationships have improved morale and encouraged teamwork at three different schools where I have served as principal."

On improving teachers' practice . . .

Publication	Project title	Relevant findings	Sample
April 2001	2001 NBCT Leadership Survey summarized in "Leading from the Classroom" An NBPTS survey conducted by Yankelovich Partners	• 99.6% of NBCTs are involved in at least one leadership role, and on average they are involved in 10 leadership activities. • 89% agree with the statement that increased involvement in leadership activities will "increase (their) effectiveness as an educator."	2186 NBCTs who achieved certification before 2000.
Fall 2001	The Impact of National Board Certification on Teachers: A Survey of NBCTs and Assessors An NBPTS survey conducted by Education Resources Group	• 64% of assessors said the experience made them more reflective about their own teaching practices. • 80% of NBCTs reported the NBC process was better than other professional development they had experienced. • 91% of NBCTs reported that NBC has positively affected their teaching practices • 83% reported that they have become more reflective about their teaching. • 69% reported positive changes in their students' engagement, achievement, and motivation.	235 NBCTs who achieved between 1994-1999 and 236 teachers who served as assessors in summer 2000 (75 of whom were NBCTs and 181 non-NBCTs)
November 2001	"I Am a Better Teacher: What Candidates for National Board Certification Say About the Assessment Process" A survey conducted by NBPTS	• 92% say they believe the NBC process has made them a better teacher. • 96% rate the NBC process as an "excellent," "very good," or "good" professional development experience. • Over 80% say the NBC process equips teachers to create stronger curricula, improves their abilities to evaluate student learning, and helps them develop a framework to use state content standards to improve teaching.	5641 first-time NBCT candidates in the 2000-2001 cycle (after completion but before notification)

Testimonials:

- Arne Duncan, chief executive, Chicago Public Schools, says, "I always meet NBCTs who tell me they didn't know how to teach before they went through this process. I think they are exaggerating—but I do know becoming an NBCT is a tremendous asset to their teaching practice."

- John Deasy, superintendent of the Santa Monica-Malibu Unified School District and former superintendent of schools in Coventry, Rhode Island, says, "I have concluded that you can't complete the process and be the same again. You will be a better teacher and obviously, if you achieve, so much the better." Reflecting on his work in Coventry, R.I., he says, "Throughout the district, we found that students generally scored higher with teachers who are National Board Certified compared to students with non-board certified teachers."

- The *Tampa Tribune and Times* wrote: "The nationwide teacher shortage isn't likely to be solved in the next few years, but there is something readily available now in Florida that can improve the quality of classroom learning while encouraging experienced teachers to mentor their newest colleagues. NBPTS offers a rigorous certification process that allows teachers to get credit for what they know and learn and how to be better in the process. School boards, superintendents and principals would do well to explore how their teachers can benefit, professionally and financially. The reward for everyone else will be in the quality of students they produce."

- Michele Forman, 2001 National Teacher of the Year, says, "As an experienced teacher, I appreciated the opportunity to examine my practice in a new and critical light. I would hope this becomes a model for the nation. I am a better teacher because of National Board Certification."

- Sharon Buddin, NASSP High School Principal of the Year, principal, Ridge View High School, Columbia, South Carolina, says, "I think National Board Certification gives teachers a chance to examine their own skills. Whether they achieve or not, it gives them a chance to analyze and improve."

Appendix B

Summary of Efforts to Improve the Quality of Teaching

	Teacher Quality Initiative	What is the rationale?	What are the assumptions?
Teachers	**1A** Teachers who want to improve their own teaching may seek out workshops and self-study resources (books, Internet, etc.) to improve their content-knowledge and pedagogical repertoire. They may be encouraged and supported to do this if resources are readily available: university partnerships, access to libraries and Internet sites, release time, etc.	Teachers will decide for themselves what they need to improve—may be based on their own reflection, feedback from an administrator, influence of school culture, etc. They will implement the changes necessary to meet those needs and cause improvement in student learning.	Teachers are able to recognize the areas of their practice that need development. Teachers will be able to connect with the resources that will effectively give them the knowledge and skills they need. The increased knowledge and skills will make these teachers more effective teachers.
School level/ principals	**2A** Schools that want to improve the quality of teaching may provide in-structional leadership (through the principal or designated teacher leaders). They will help teachers to identify what they need to do to improve the quality of their teaching, and they will provide the training and resources to do it.	Administrators will provide instructional leadership. Teachers will make suggested changes or learn to use new strategies through provided training and resources. The changes will cause an improve-ment in student learning.	Administrators have the knowledge and skill they need to provide instructional leadership, to diagnose instructional needs, and prescribe training and resources. Teachers will value and honor the suggestions of their administrators. Administrators will be able to identify and provide necessary training and resources. Teachers will effectively make the changes and/ or integrate the new practices into their repertoires.

cont.

	Teacher Quality Initiative	What is the rationale?	What are the assumptions?
School level/ principals *cont.*	**2B** Schools that want to improve the quality of teaching may also work to develop a strong culture of collegiality, a community of learning.	The strong culture of collegiality created and sustained by administrators will enable teachers to see each other as resources and work together on common problems to make a greater impact on student learning.	Administrators and teachers know how to create and sustain a strong culture. The improved culture will help teachers to improve the quality of teaching that they can provide.
	2C Schools that want to improve the quality of teaching may demonstrate quality teaching by showing videotapes or coordinating peer observations.	Teachers will effectively implement observed teaching strategies; this will help them build their own repertoires so that they can have more options as they work to meet the needs of each child and improve student learning.	Teachers will be able to "pick up" strategies by observing them; they will know when the strategies are appropriate and for whom.
District level	**3A** Districts that want to improve the quality of teaching might establish teacher evaluation benchmarks by which to reward or sanction teaching quality.	Teachers will align their teaching practice to these benchmarks in response to rewards or sanctions. The benchmarks are based upon standards that will improve student learning.	Teachers will know how to align their teaching to the benchmarks. They will have the training and resources they need to do so. There is a rationale for why teaching practice aligned to the benchmarks will lead to improved learning. Evaluators will effectively evaluate teaching performances based on the benchmarks.
	3B Districts that want to improve the quality of teaching might provide professional development (PD) programming/time for the teachers in the district.	This professional development time will provide opportunities for teachers to gain the information and theory on content, pedagogy, and child development that they need to improve student learning.	The professional development will address the areas teachers need. The PD will effectively enable teachers to gain new knowledge and skills and to know when to use them.

	Teacher Quality Initiative	What is the rationale?	What are the assumptions?
State level	**4A** States that want to improve the quality of teaching might try to control the quality of teaching through initial and professional licensure regulations.	Control over teaching licensure will weed out people who are deemed to have little potential to be high-quality teachers who can improve student learning.	Some people can't be high-quality teachers and these people can be identified.
	4B States that want to improve the quality of teaching might try to provide rewards (teacher bonuses, school recognition) and sanctions (probation status, withholding student diplomas) to teachers and their teaching contexts.	Rewards and sanctions will motivate teachers to meet the requirements; requirements are based on standards that will improve student learning.	The rewards and sanctions will be sufficiently motivating for teachers to make changes in their teaching. The standards for judgment are correlated to improved student learning. The sanction/reward system accommodates the fact that some students are "harder" or "easier" to teach.
	4C States that want to improve the quality of teaching might try to impose learning standards for what students should know and be able to do.	The standards provide a common high benchmark for all; teachers will teach to these new standards and this will improve student learning.	Teachers will have the knowledge and skills to teach the content of the standards. Teachers will have the resources (time and materials) to teach the content of the standards. Teachers will agree to teach the content of the standards.
	4D States that want to improve the quality of teaching might allow charter schools to form so that market forces of competition will give teachers a reason to change.	Ingrained school structures and state regulations are in the way of improved student learning; remove them and innovate to improve student learning.	The innovations will have better outcomes.

	Teacher Quality Initiative	What is the rationale?	What are the assumptions?
Federal level	**5A** The federal government wanted to improve the quality of teaching for disenfranchised students (students with disabilities, limited English proficiency, or who need compensatory education) so they passed laws.	Legislation will guarantee the right for disenfranchised people to have the opportunity for education. Schools that do not comply can be sued if they do not increase opportunities for student learning.	Parents will know the extent of their child's rights and will sue when their children are not receiving the services they deserve.
	6B The federal government wants to improve the quality of teaching for all students so it has tied funding to assessment. (No Child Left Behind)	States who want access to special government funding will comply with the law; they will test all students every year and create sanctions for schools that do not make adequate yearly progress in student achievement gains. The sanctions will be an incentive and the funding will provide the means for districts to provide what is needed to improve student learning.	All states will want the funding. The assessment will represent a valid indication of what the assessment set out to test, and it will give accurate results that will fairly gauge student progress. School districts will know what is needed to improve student learning.
	6C The federal government wants to improve the quality of teaching. It has supported the establishment of a National Board for Professional Teaching Standards, which has developed a new industry standard for "what teachers should know and be able to do."	Teacher quality is the most important influence on student learning. Combine the rigor of research with the wisdom of practice to define "quality teaching"; then focus all teacher quality initiatives on these standards which have been known and shown to improve student learning.	"Quality teaching" can be defined and identified. The standards of quality teaching will lead to high levels of student learning. Teachers who are identified by the quality of their teaching will be used to support related reforms.

	Teacher Quality Initiative	What is the rationale?	What are the assumptions?
The Public	**6A** Citizens who want to improve the quality of teaching for their disenfranchised children can sue the government.	The U.S. Supreme Court guaranteed that the opportunity of an education is "a right which must be available to all on equal terms" in Brown vs. Board of Education Legislation exists which protects this right. Adults who know their rights can sue when the rights of children are violated.	There are parents, caregivers, or organizations that know their rights, know that they are being violated, and have the resources to sue on behalf of the child or group of children.
	6B Community members who want to improve the quality of teaching might make the work that schools do more visible.	When the successes and failures of schools are made transparent (through the news media, public reporting, or community participation in the school), schools will have an incentive to avoid the failures and strive to succeed in improving student learning.	Schools will be represented fairly by the media and other reporting measures. Schools will have the knowledge, skills, and resources they need to succeed/avoid failure.
	6C Business community members who want to improve the quality of teaching so that they will have a stronger work force might contribute time, money, and other resources to education.	The business community has resources that will be useful in enabling other initiatives to succeed. These initiatives are aimed at improving student learning.	The barrier to other initiatives' success is a lack of resources. Business community members (working with educators) will know how to best allocate these resources.

Appendix C

A Guide to Videotaping
By Matthew M. Delaney, NBCT

Introduction

There are few segments of the National Board Certification process that appear to intimidate candidates more than the requirement that they videotape selected segments of teaching practice as a portion of two portfolio entries. Many excellent teachers waste valuable time and energy trying to devise an ideal classroom environment for videotaping when their efforts would be better spent establishing and maintaining an ideal environment for learning—the classroom. The optimal classroom setting for the videotaped entries, then, is the one documenting the authentic comments and responses, curriculum, and classroom layout where you—as instructional leader and facilitator of learning—teach every day. The video camera should be considered a valuable tool employed in a genuine effort to critically describe, analyze, and reflect upon teaching and learning. And, it is one from which all teachers may profit.

As a skilled and concerned educator, you begin each day prepared to challenge, effectively engage, and provide ongoing support for your students—all of your students. In the same way that you adapt the presentation and application of the knowledge and skills required to increase achievement for all learners, consider the optimal ways in which you can visually illustrate the consistent application of active teaching and learning that take place within your classroom. The point here is not to change what it is that you show the National Board assessors; but, more importantly, show what it is that you do.

The videotaped entries differ markedly from the other portfolio entries in the focus of their concern. The written commentary in the other portfolio entries describes and supports your collaborations with colleagues, with students and parents, with administrators, and with the community through which you interact within the multidimensional fabric of teaching. The video entries are more specifically about you. They present you and your students within faithful visual documentations that provide "essential evidence" of your teaching practice.

As a candidate for National Board Certification, you should think of your videotaped entries as windows whereby assessors may observe and evaluate accomplished teaching. For the National Board assessors, these videos are the only views they will see that will paint brief pictures from two selected samples of your day-to-day teaching. Together with your commentaries, the video entries can offer an authentic and complete representation of your role as a leader of learning. You should consider that this is the closest assessors will come to your classroom without actually meeting with you and your students directly.

Another important function of videotaped classroom observations comes from its use as a mirror providing reflections of professional practice. As a National Board Certified Teacher Candidate, the videotapes allow you to preview the lessons that you anticipate using in your portfolio entries, and to observe reflected views of you and your students from a new and different perspective. If you have not used videotaped analysis of your teaching before, you will discover that it will prove to be a valuable teaching and learning experience.

Although you should not let technical concerns misdirect you from the real value of the videotaped sequences, these entries and the accompanying commentaries are serious business. The videotapes that you submit serve to function as rich resources that are used to assess the learning climate in your classroom, how your students interact among themselves and with you, and the ways in which you engage your students. They also provide information regarding the impact of your teaching on student learning as well as the ways in which you manage, even during these brief observations, the day-to-day issues of teaching.

In order to enable the assessors to provide you with the most equitable evaluation for each of your portfolio entries, it is exceedingly important that each candidate review the requirements for his or her particular certification area. The directions are very specific and you must do exactly what the directions ask you to do. Although this guide addresses videotaping, you should also consider where the video entries fit within the overall themes and concepts presented in each of your lessons for the portfolio entries.

Through your videotapes, you are encouraged to demonstrate the complexity, the depth of learning, and the content integration across the curriculum that you employ in your instructional practice. In the same way that one-shot and single-concept professional development are ineffective for improving teaching performance, do not expect to make your video-taped entries one-shot or single-concept efforts to portray learning experiences for students. Including videotaping as a part of the daily instructional process will help to make you feel more at ease and in control of your classroom performance. Your students, too, act more naturally in front of the camera if they have the opportunity to become used to its presence in class. So, consider videotaping to be a skill that can be developed and improved over time. You will be most successful when you practice, videotape often, and select the segments that best display your accomplished professional practice in the classroom.

For your information, there are some conditions that apply to all certificate areas. You should be aware, however, that the requirements for the kinds of classroom practice required in each certificate field may, and often do, vary. This is particularly true in subjects that are considered outside of the "core academic" areas. Each certificate also specifies the following: the length of the videotaped segments, whether the video shows you facilitating student performance in a situation requiring demonstrated applications related to subject content, your leadership in full class instruction, your involvement with a single learner, or your engagement of and interactions with a specified number of learners in small group instruction.

Permission/Release Forms

Before you begin videotaping, make certain that you have obtained appropriate permission from the parent or guardian of every student.

The National Board for Professional Teaching Standards requires that you secure a general permission from each of your students to cover all of the taping as needed, including practice. You must also obtain permission from any adults who may appear in your video. You should send a letter explaining the importance of your involvement in the National Board Certification process along with the release form. This would be a good time to impress upon the parent(s) or guardian(s) an understanding that National Board Certification is the most advanced level of certification available in the teaching profession. You may express your confidence in the classwork of their child as you include artifacts and videos in your portfolio entries and welcome their questions or comments. If, for some reason, a student's parent or guardian refuses to grant permission, then, of course, you don't want to make an issue of the student's inability to participate in the class. Just make sure that he or she is seated outside the camera's view for all videotaping sessions. Anyone operating the camera for you should also be aware of this and any other limitations that may be imposed during the videotaping of the class.

The National Board has provided release forms for your use, and they can be found at the end of each portfolio section. These sections have an **Adult Release Form** and a **Student Release Form** in both English and Spanish. They are in the portfolio materials provided by NBPTS. In addition, your school or program policy may require certain releases and provide their own forms. Be sure that you know what is required for your school or district. To confirm that you have obtained, and maintain on file, permission for all students who appear in the videotapes, you will need to sign the **Teacher Release Form.**

Technical Issues

Some of the technical requirements are very specific; they must be strictly adhered to and apply to all video entries.

You should review the instructions for your particular certificate for a detailed description of the specific requirements for your portfolio entries.

Videotaped segments must not extend beyond the *specified time allowed.*

If your videotape is longer than the requirement for the portfolio entry requirement, it will not be viewed by the assessors beyond the time specified in your portfolio directions for that entry. Since 10, or 15, or 20 minutes is a very short period of time in an instructional sequence, some teachers find it difficult to select what they perceive as an uninterrupted segment that provides the highpoints of the videotaped classroom activity. You may want to ask the opinion of a colleague who is familiar with your subject and teaching. However, in the long run, you are the best judge of what is occurring in the classroom and how it meets the requirements for the entry. View your videotapes over and over. The more familiar you are with the action and response in the classroom, the better able you will be to judge its value and comment and reflect upon it.

All videotapes you prepare must be *continuous* and *unedited.*

This means that you are asked to keep the camera running for the full duration of a lesson, without turning it off and back on. Do not stop and restart the camera during any portion of the submitted videotaped sequence. Stopping and restarting the audio portion is also considered to be an edit of the tape. If you change the position of the camera or the microphone, the move must be included as a continuous part of the videotaped segment. You should consider that it is an unavoidable part of the documentary nature of the recording. The assessors understand this, and it will not affect your score. Make sure that anyone who assists you with your entry fully understands this requirement.

Videotapes must be recorded from a *single camera.*

If you comply with the requirement that the videotapes be continuous and unedited, this should not be an issue for you.

Videotapes must *not* include any form of *audio and/or video en-hancement, manipulation, or graphics,* including voice-overs, captions, music, repeat scenes, motion effects, fades, split screens, and so on.

Many cameras, even inexpensive models, now provide a range of selections and controls that allow amateur videographers to enhance home videos. For the purposes of documenting classroom practice for submission to the National Board, however, special effects are not allowed. This requirement is important for candidates to strictly adhere to because manipulated tapes are difficult for scorers to interpret and can misrepresent or distort the true character of the events.

Keep in mind that the National Board guidelines allow that your score can only reflect the direct evidence that you present in your submitted entry. The scoring rubrics for each entry are centered on your ability to provide clear, consistent, and convincing evidence of accomplished practice based on the National Board Standards for your certificate. Your score is not determined by measuring the professional level of your video presentation. However, your score is determined by your ability to demonstrate that you meet the Standards for Accomplished Teaching: that you employ quality teaching strategies; that you present your ability to engage students in meaningful interactive learning experiences; and that you describe, analyze, evaluate, and reflect upon the contextual significance of the videotaped evidence within the National Board Standards.

 Note: Except when instructed to do so in an entry (such as transferring two segments onto a single tape), your tapes should contain no breaks in the video footage. **This is important: Not following these guidelines will result, at a minimum, in a reduction of your score and may make your entry unscoreable.**

Videotapes must be submitted in standard VHS format.

Since the various derivations of the 8mm format are currently the most popular on the market, you may find it more convenient to videotape in a miniature format such as 8mm, Hi8mm, Digital-8, or VHS-C formats. Regardless of the format of the original, your submitted tapes must be copied, if necessary, and submitted in standard VHS format. Consumer demand drives the electronics market and people want high quality in a smaller and lighter package and at a lower overall cost. Since full-size cameras that use standard VHS format tapes are becoming less popular due to their large size and weight, they are becoming increasingly difficult to find. The smaller, more convenient formats, therefore, are readily available and should present little difficulty for even a novice to use.

Actually, the range of 8mm formats currently available record superior video and audio content compared to the earlier standard VHS technologies and should also be preferred over the VHS-C format. VHS-C, although compact in size, records on a limited-length videotape. The one convenience of the VHS-C cassette is that it can be installed in an adapter and inserted for use in a standard VHS playback deck. However, tapes in adapters are not allowed for submission by the NBPTS, and VHS-C copies are generally inferior to the 8mm formats. Among the 8mm cameras, all of the brands available on the market produce quality units at affordable prices. And, best of all, the newer cameras have enlarged viewing screens, often have the capability to record both video and stills, and even novices can produce quality results.

Purchase or borrow a good-quality tripod.

While you are considering ways to create effective videotaped records of accomplished practice, one of the best accessories to assist you in that effort is a quality tripod. Good tripods are expensive, often costing well over $100, but they protect your video camera by providing a stronger "footprint" and they allow a smoother range of motion for anyone recording classroom action for you. Also, many high-quality tripods allow easy mounting and dismounting of the camera through the use of a sliding "shoe" that will simplify your efforts to videotape on your own.

Safeguard your tape.

Nearly all 8mm, Hi8, and Digital-8 cameras contain playback functions and can be easily connected to a standard VHS deck.

☞   **Important:** You must provide the title and your candidate ID number on the videotape. Once you are convinced that you have an acceptable classroom videotape, safeguard your efforts and break off the safety tab on the back of the videocassette. Then make a quality copy for your files.

You should break off the safety tab for your original videotape as well as for any copies that you make. If you decide that you want to tape over any of the tapes again, it is easy to restore the record function by replacing the missing safety tab with a piece of tape, allowing re-recording. However, to save you valuable time and concern and to prevent an accidental erasure during playback and/or recording of a portfolio entry, take this protective step of removing the safety tab on your classroom videotapes.

Videotape segments are intended to document and provide an authentic illustration of teaching and learning.

Student interaction and response are the essential element in successful videotapes. Select a camera angle that will show as many of the students' faces as possible. If you have a person operating the camera for you, make sure that he or she understands this point. If the camera operator focuses in on one child or a small group of students, either by moving the camera or through careful and judicious use of the zoom function, stress the importance of maintaining a view that clearly shows facial features and student responses.

Although it is a significant advantage to have a knowledgeable adult operate the camera for you, often a talented student can operate the camera very well. Students are well acquainted with the physical layout of the room and the lesson as well as the classroom dynamics to which an outsider cannot readily relate. It would not be fair, however, to use a student in this capacity if this filming responsibility denies him or her irreplaceable participation and learning time. This is a decision that only you can make.

It is also possible for the NBCT candidate to place the video camera on a tripod and videotape his or her own class. Sometimes it is not possible to arrange for a camera operator at a particular time. If you are in a situation where it becomes necessary to videotape your own classes, begin the tape in the widest (numerically small) zoom or focal length setting on the lens that the camera provides. You should try to place the camera high and to one side, possibly on a countertop or a table, so that the camera will record the facial features and actions of as many students as possible.

☞ **Remember**, the videotapes that you produce for your portfolio entries are not for general entertainment; they are evidence of accomplished practice.

You may record a portion of the videotape with the camera on a tripod, and then, either move the tripod closer to the students or hand-hold the camera for a portion of the time so that you can walk around the room to capture authentic student responses. If you are moving the field of view—panning—across a group of students from one side to another, be very careful. You must move the camera slowly to allow a natural and fluid recording of information. *Never* move the camera back and forth to follow a conversation. If necessary, move the camera to include both students in a part of the viewing field, or just videotape one student as you either zoom out or move the camera away from the group to show a wider view of the class. Too much camera motion can seriously detract from the ability of the assessors to observe expressions and actions in the class. Once again, make certain that the camera is never stopped and records continuously as you move the camera throughout the class.

Audio—the sound portion of your videotape—must be intelligible in order to provide assessors with an understanding of all that you say and as much as possible of what your students say.

The requirement that the audio portion of the tape be clearly understood really goes hand-in-hand with your efforts to produce an authentic document that is a valid representation of your classroom lesson. Clear voices will reinforce the accompanying commentary and improve the ability of the National Board assessors to fairly assess your entry.

All cameras have built-in microphones, so it is easy to assume that sound is being recorded at the same quality level as video. However, the quality of the sound that the microphone on the camera records has no relationship to the quality of the image that is recorded on the videotape. The microphone has been designed to perform under a range of conditions that often may not be ideal for the classroom documentation of portfolio entries. The built-in microphone is designed to provide a function that automatically levels all sound impulses coming into the microphone. What that means to you is that the camera is trying to balance anything that you or anyone near you may say with sounds and voices from all corners of the room. Your voice and the voices of your students may not only be competing with each other but they may also be competing with shuffled papers, a tapping pencil, the fan for the heat or air conditioner, the AV presentation in the next room, or any other noticeable sound source. These unwanted noises may cause the resultant audio recording to be misleading or even unintelligible when played back.

What you really want is to be able to direct and contain the sound pattern or area where voices are recorded. There are a number of easy and inexpensive ways to do this. Much of the quality of your sound recording depends on the physical layout and appointments of your classroom. If you have low ceilings, a relatively square room, and a carpeted floor, you may have little difficulty recording acceptable audio quality. However, even the number of students in the class can have a pronounced effect on the sound quality. For most teaching situations, though, it is better to use a supplemental sound device such as a PZM microphone rather than the built-in camera microphone.

A PZM microphone, also known as a pressure zone microphone, is relatively inexpensive and readily available ($50 to $70 at an electronics store). There are other types of microphones that will also work well, but make sure that you explain to the salesperson what the intended use is for the microphone. Some microphones require phantom power (outside power source) to work, and probably are not worth the effort or investment to adequately serve your needs. Most PZM microphones look like small ping-pong paddles and lie flat to pick up the sounds that reflect off of large reflecting surfaces, such as tabletops or walls. These microphones can be moved with the camera and taped to a chalkboard or tabletop to improve the recording of primary sound impulses. The chief advantage of a PZM microphone is its ability to eliminate most secondary sources such as echoes and extraneous noises.

For almost all video cameras, the external PZM microphone is plugged into the "EXT MIC" jack on the camera. Most PZM microphones will come with an assortment of adapters to work with different cameras. If yours does not have the appropriate adapter, you can purchase one at an electronics store.

When plugged in, the built-in microphone automatically turns off and only the sounds from the external microphone will be recorded.

Be sure to check this feature of your camera before you begin taping and make sure that the external microphone is working. If the microphone is incorrectly connected, or if the battery is weak or dead, the sound will not be recorded on your videotape. You will need headphones to monitor the external sound coming into the camera.

Boundary microphones are comparable to PZM microphones with respect to the area in which they optimally record sound, and although superior to the on-camera mike, they actually employ conventional sound technology and create audio patterns similar to other external microphones. They can, however, be moved around to record group interactions that help to clarify and reinforce information that is recorded on the videotape. Other microphones such as a lavaliere, which can be worn on a collar or tie, or an omnidirectional handheld unit may improve the sound over what you can record with the on-camera mike. However, don't forget that your primary concern should be directed toward teaching and your technical concerns should help and not hinder that effort.

So, your first choice should be to try to find a PZM microphone. Crown produces the Sound Grabber II that has proved to provide superior classroom recording of large and small groups. The now-discontinued Radio Shack PZM microphone is also excellent, but may be difficult to find. Peavey and Audio Technica produce quality microphones, but they are generally expensive and, since they require phantom power, are difficult to use with most current equipment. Some of the major electronics chain stores also sell PZM microphones. You may have to check to see if any stores in your local area stock this item. If not, there are many retailers on the Internet that can provide the Crown Sound Grabber II at discount prices.

If you are doing the recording yourself, check the sound quality with headphones—if you have a cameraperson, ask him or her to wear headphones.

It is important to monitor the sound during videotaping and to rectify audio problems as they occur. Remember, if you do not have a cameraperson and are running the video camera from a tripod placement, it is very important that you check and double-check to make sure that the microphone is operating properly before you begin videotaping the lesson. If you record without sound, your tape will be unscoreable.

Copying and Duplication

The portfolio entries require you to transfer two or more segments of video footage onto a single tape to be submitted for assessment. You should also make essential backup copies of the videotapes that you are submitting to keep for yourself. The videotapes that you send in with your portfolio will not be returned to you.

In order to transfer video segments onto one tape, and to make a backup copy of your tape, you will need:

- **Two VCRs** (one for playback and one for recording) or a camera that allows playback and has AUDIO and VIDEO output jacks that allow you to record to an auxiliary VCR.
- **Cables** to connect the two VCRs or a camera and VCR (generally RCA type connectors)
- **A TV**
- **Blank VHS videotapes**

Set up the two VCRs or the camera and VCR by connecting the AUDIO/OUT from the playback VCR or camera to the AUDIO/IN plug on the VCR used for recording. Then, connect the VIDEO/OUT from the playback VCR or camera to the VIDEO/IN plug on the VCR used for recording. Last, attach the playback VCR to the TV by connecting the VCR's CABLE/OUT plug to the TV's ANTENNA or CABLE/IN plug. It may also be helpful to consult the specific instructions that came with the VCR and camera or to get technical assistance from the audio-visual (AV) resource person in your district for the transfer and duplication of videotapes.

When you record, make sure that the recording deck is set to the high-quality recording speed setting. If your VCR provides SP, which stands for standard play, and EP, which stands for extended play, you want the SP setting. The EP setting creates too much distortion when copying video-tapes and may produce unacceptable results. Your video camera may also have an EDIT function switch that enhances the signal when in the copy mode. Check the manual for any special features or procedures that may be unique to your equipment.

Finally, make sure that you clearly label your videotape. **You must provide the title and your candidate ID number.** This is also a good time to break off the safety tab on the back of the VHS cassette to protect all of your hard work. Of course, you should safeguard your original videotape by clearly marking it and placing it in a secure location. It would also be to your advantage at this time to make a quality copy of the correctly timed and sequenced entry material that you have submitted to the National Board for Professional Teaching Standards.

Checklist

Camera and tapes—Use the best-quality equipment available to you. Check with your district, school, department, parents, and/or community organizations for sources of high-quality equipment.

VHS videotapes—Use new videotapes of high quality from a recognized manufacturer to provide you with the best possible recording quality.

Tripod—Use of a sturdy tripod will allow you to keep the camera steady, especially for long periods of time.

Extension cord—Electronic cable lengths vary for the microphone as well as for the AC power adapter for the camera. The microphone extension cord will allow more freedom of movement in the classroom. The AC power adapter will eliminate the possibility of losing power in the middle of a taping session due to weak batteries. If, however, you must use battery power, check that batteries are fully charged and have a spare battery available.

Headphones—Use headphones to perform a sound check every time that you intend to use the camera and to monitor the sound being recorded.

PZM microphone—An external Pressure Zone Microphone (PZM) can be placed near students and connected to the camera over long distances to optimize recordings.

Cameraperson—It is strongly recommended that you find a cameraperson to assist you. Although it is possible to set up and control the camera yourself, having a cameraperson leaves you free to concentrate on your teaching. The cameraperson needs to be competent, willing, and available to film multiple sessions until you get what you want. He or she needs to be familiar with the equipment you are using and the unique challenges of classroom videotaping. You will need to get together and talk about your plans for the lesson, what you anticipate students will be doing, how students might be grouped or moving around, and the specific skills or issues you want to demonstrate on the videotape for each entry.

Practice—Practice, practice, practice. In order to create a natural-appearing classroom video that captures your best teaching, practice is essential. When a video camera is in the classroom for the first time, students and teachers behave differently. Some students may become quiet while others wave and play to the camera. You may not appear the way you think you do in real life. You may discover that you repeat words, do not clearly enunciate, make the same movement again and again, or tend to call on the same students. Yet, videotaping is incidental to the real business of the classroom—which is teaching. It should be valued for what it can provide for you—it is a valuable tool that can and should be employed to continually improve your teaching skills effectiveness in the classroom.

Additional Reminders

Always keep the microphone close to the action. The location of the microphone is key to capturing quality audio. If you are not using an external microphone, the camera will have to move to the areas of interest for the on-camera microphone to record the best sound fidelity.

Be sure that all cables are secured. If necessary, use duct tape (silver fabric-backed tape) or masking tape to hold cables in place. Many audio problems are not the fault of the equipment quality but of faulty connections.

A general rule is to keep the camera still and make changes sparingly. When videotaping, fewer camera movements such as zooming in and out result in more viewable video. Use camera motion sparingly. When a change of view is made, hold that view for several seconds. Never try to follow a conversation or sequenced action repeatedly back and forth between two or more subjects. If the camera does pan (moving from left to right or right to left), it must be very slow and smooth. Too much motion makes the videotape uncomfortable to watch and difficult to score.

It is better, generally, to maintain a wide angle than to zoom in and show close-up shots. Wide-angle shots provide the advantage of exhibiting better classroom context and capturing more action rather than less. Recording too close to the subjects in the videotape often does not allow sufficient space for the give-and-take that is part of the normal classroom activity.

Zoom in for close-up shots. Hold long enough so that viewers can see the item being talked about, pointed at, or read what is being shown. Make sure, however, that the microphone is correctly employed and the sound matches the visual image. It is important that scorers are able to understand the conversation. If written material must be videotaped as part of a classroom instructional sequence, it may be useful to use large sheets of paper or a chart or conference pad and a large marker. Information can be recorded without glare and reflections that will be distracting in the videotaped segment.

Show the faces and hands of students and the teacher. Expressions and gestures show the impact of teaching and the involvement in learning among the students. For this reason, you should plan your camera placement to avoid the back of anyone's head for any extended period of time.

Avoid placing people in front of bright lights. Windows, overhead projectors, and computer screens create silhouettes and hide facial expressions. It is important to have adequate lighting. Attempt to select light source(s) above and to the front of the subjects. Make sure that all lights are on in the room and if you use window lighting, make sure it does not distract from recording important features and responses.

Some portfolio entries require that you start the videotaping session by taking a slow pan of the room. A 3-second pan for each 45 degrees that you pass through and not exceeding 1 minute total will provide a sense of where things are located in your room, including students, tables, materials, and so forth. Linger on those things that are interesting to provide a stronger visual reference for scorers. Check with the specific requirements for your certificate area.

Review video footage. Once you have practiced videotaping and have completed one or more taping sessions with your class, you will need to sit down and review your video footage to consider how different parts illustrate how your teaching reflects the Standards for your certificate. Take notes and mark the footage each time you view the tape to help you point out and return to particular elements in the videotape for your commentary. If, after reviewing the tapes, you decide that you are not satisfied with either the technical quality or the examples of your teaching, you may decide to videotape additional lessons. This is a good reason why you should **videotape early and often.**

Review video segments in collaboration with a colleague. When selecting the final video segments for your portfolio, a colleague who is familiar with your content area or the learning challenges presented in delivering comprehensive instruction for your particular group of students may be able to provide unique and valuable perspectives. You may also find that enlisting the assistance of another teacher may help you in your own evaluation of the process of teaching that is reflected in the videotapes.

Use the National Board for Professional Teaching Standards comprehensive materials and resources. NBPTS offers a wide range of products, resources, and services intended to provide support for National Board Certification in your certificate area. One of the most useful resources is in the portfolio provided to you in your NBPTS portfolio. The **NBPTS Analysis Questions and the Analysis into Action/ Course of Action Form** will provide excellent guidance as you address the commentaries directed toward your videotape portfolio entries.

Final Thoughts

The video entries often produce unnecessary anxiety for NBCT candidates. Take a deep breath and relax. You will **not** be scored on the technical quality of your video, and you are **not** expected to produce broadcast-quality video. The intent of the entry is to provide evidence of high-quality teaching and learning in your classroom based on the Standards and Core Propositions for the National Board for Professional Teaching Standards. For that reason, you will want to present yourself in the best possible manner. Good things in teaching do not always occur on demand and when they do occur, they can often be difficult to capture on videotape. This guide attempts to provide helpful hints for videotaping to make the process a little less stressful and easier to manage.

Appendix D

Web-based Resources

By Jill Harrison Berg, NBCT
and Martha Bosco, NBCT

The following pages provide a listing of some Web-based professional and logistical resources that candidates, candidate support facilitators, and NBCTs may find useful as they support one another and seek new roles.

Links to Professional Associations

Professional Associations exist in education in a variety of subject areas, developmental levels, and specialty areas. These professional associations play the important role of connecting relevant research to practice, coordinating and archiving the knowledge base, and advocating for high-quality teaching and learning in that field. Teachers who are concerned about improving the quality of their teaching practice and who want to influence teaching culture should take the initiative to get involved in one or more of these associations through its national chapter or regional affiliates.

While membership has its benefits, most of the Web sites of these associations provide free access to useful resources for nonmembers as well.

National Council of Teachers of English
http://www.ncte.org/
The National Council of Teachers of English (NCTE) is one of the oldest and largest professional associations in education. Since 1911 it has been devoted to "improving the teaching of English and the language arts at all levels of education." Through conventions, journals, online resources, and other publications, NCTE provides resources that are useful for all teachers of English.

National Council for the Social Studies
http://www.ncss.org/
The National Council for the Social Studies (NCSS) "engages and supports educators in strengthening and advocating social studies." This umbrella organization serves social studies teachers in all areas and in many specializations including elementary, secondary, and college teachers of history, geography, economics, political science, sociology, psychology, anthropology, and law-related education. Visit the Web site to learn about state, local, and national affiliates, and for information on grants, professional opportunities, teaching resources, and much more.

National Center for History in the Schools
http://www.sscnet.ucla.edu/nchs/
This site is produced by UCLA's Social Sciences Division to promote quality history education. It provides learning standards, research guides, lesson plans, resource recommendations, and links.

National Council of Teachers of Mathematics
http://www.nctm.org/
The National Council of Teachers of Mathematics (NCTM) "offers vision, leadership, and avenues of communication for mathematics educators" for teachers at all levels. Visit the Web site to learn about regional and national conferences, and to access resources such as lessons linked to the NCTM standards, grant opportunities, and professional development ideas.

National Science Teachers Association
http://www.nsta.org/
The National Science Teachers Association (NSTA) is "committed to promoting excellence and innovation in science teaching and learning for all." NSTA's work is enriched by a membership that includes more than 53,000 science teachers, science supervisors, administrators, scientists, business and industry representatives, and others involved in science education. The Web site is well-designed, easy to navigate, and full of resources for teachers, parents, students, and administrators.

American Association for the Advancement of Science
http://www.aaas.org/
The American Association for the Advancement of Science (AAAS) is the world's largest general scientific society and the publisher of *Science* magazine. In 1985 it founded Project 2061 "to help all Americans become literate in science, mathematics, and technology." It is well-known for its landmark publication *Science for All Americans* which can be accessed at http://www.project2061.org/.

American Library Association

http://www.ala.org/

The American Library Association (ALA) "provides leadership for the development, promotion, and improvement of library and information services and the profession of librarianship in order to enhance learning and ensure access to information for all." The rich resources of this organization and this Web site serve more than 100,000 libraries across the United States.

International Reading Association

www.reading.org

The International Reading Association (IRA) is "a professional membership organization dedicated to promoting high levels of literacy for all by improving the quality of reading instruction, disseminating research and information about reading, and encouraging the lifetime reading habit." The IRA provides resources aimed to advance its mission to its members in 99 countries. The IRA also works in partnership with the National Council of Teachers of English (NCATE) to accredit programs in reading and has its own "Standards for Reading Professionals," which will interest National Board Certification candidates who teach English.

National Art Education Association

http://www.naea-reston.org/

The goal of the National Art Education Association (NAEA) is to "promote art education through professional development, service, advancement of knowledge, and leadership." The Web site offers up-to-date information about contests, legislative alerts, and newly released resources. Unique features include downloadable art advocacy materials and a visual arts education research agenda.

Music Teachers National Association

http://www.mtna.org/

The Music Teachers National Association (MTNA) is committed to "advancing the value of music study and music making to society and to supporting the professionalism of music teachers." This beautiful site takes a few minutes to load, but it is well worth it. (Make sure your sound is turned on!) Music teachers will appreciate this rich space in which they can connect with other professionals and professional resources. Note that MTNA has its own "national certification" program.

American Alliance for Health, Physical Education, Recreation and Dance

http://www.aahperd.org/

The American Alliance for Health, Physical Education, Recreation and Dance (AAHPERD) is "an alliance of six national associations and six district associations and is designed to provide members with a comprehensive and coordinated array of resources, support, and programs to help practitioners improve their skills and so further the health and well-being of the American public." The Web site provides easy links to the affiliated associations (national and regional) and offers resources such as an online journal, a media center, and an opinion forum.

International Society for Technology in Education
http://www.iste.org/
The International Society for Technology in Education (ISTE) is dedicated to "promoting appropriate uses of information technology to support and improve learning, teaching, and administration in K–12 education and teacher education." Enriched by membership from all over the globe, this Web site is packed with rich resources including online tools, support for building business partnerships, networking opportunities, and guidance for the challenges teachers face in incorporating computers, the Internet, and other new technologies into their schools.

National Association for Bilingual Education
http://www.nabe.org/
The National Association for Bilingual Education (NABE) was established in 1975 "to address the educational needs of language-minority students in the United States and to advance the language competencies and multicultural understanding of all Americans." The only national organization focused exclusively on the needs of language-minority students, NABE is both a professional and advocacy association. Its members include educators, parents, community members, and leaders of community, governmental, and business organizations. The site has useful links, discussion forums, and legislative action alerts.

American Educational Research Association
http://www.aera.net/
The American Educational Research Association (AERA) is "concerned with improving the educational process by encouraging scholarly inquiry related to education and by promoting the dissemination and practical application of research results." This giant international professional organization hosts a Web site full of information on professional development opportunities, fellowships and grants, and, of course, research.

American Federation of Teachers
http://www.aft.org/
The American Federation of Teachers (AFT) is one of the two largest professional associations in education. The AFT Web site has a variety of resources that teachers will find useful from news updates, to information on conferences, grants, and programs, to position papers on many important and

timely issues. It also has a special page with resources and information about National Board Certification: http://www.aft.org/edissues/teacherquality/evalnbpts.htm.

National Education Association
http://www.nea.org/

The National Education Association (NEA) is education's oldest and largest professional organization. Since 1857 the NEA has been "committed to advancing the cause of public education." The NEA Web site has information about member services, legislative action, and special events. The "Hot Topics" section provides overviews and links for various education topics including National Board Certification. The NEA also supports improved teaching and learning through OWL.org.

OWL.org—Our Web Location for Education
http://www.owl.org/

OWL.org is "an online community where educators can connect to share their knowledge and experience." The National Education Association provides this free service in partnership with several partners including Public Broadcasting System (PBS), the Association for Supervision and Curriculum Development (ASCD), Teachers-Teachers.com, Education World, and others. The site features online discussions, archives full of resources for teachers, and special offers and discounts from partner organizations.

National Middle School Association
http://www.nmsa.org/

The National Middle School Association (NMSA) "serves as a voice for professionals, parents, and others interested in the educational and developmental needs of young adolescents (youth 10–15 years of age)." Teachers of young adolescents will welcome the attention to the unique needs of early adolescents which NMSA journals, conferences, and resources provide. Particularly useful are the links to relevant research. National Board Certification candidates for Early Adolescence (EA) certificates should take the time to browse here.

National Association for Developmental Education
http://www.nade.net/

The National Association for Developmental Education (NADE) "seeks to improve the theory and practice of developmental education in postsecondary education, the professional capabilities of developmental educators, and the design of programs to prepare developmental educators." Teachers who want to know more about developmental education and how to design instruction with developmental needs in mind will find the links this site provides useful.

National Association for the Education of Young Children
http://www.naeyc.org/default.htm
The National Association for the Education of Young Children (NAEYC) is "dedicated to improving the quality of early childhood education programs for children from birth through age 8." National Board Certification candidates for Early Childhood/Generalist (EC/GEN) should take the time to browse here.

Council for Exceptional Children
http://www.cec.sped.org/
The Council for Exceptional Children (CEC) is "the largest international professional organization dedicated to improving educational outcomes for individuals with exceptionalities, students with disabilities, and/or the gifted. CEC advocates for appropriate governmental policies, sets professional standards, provides continual professional development, advocates for newly and historically underserved individuals with exceptionalities, and helps professionals obtain conditions and resources necessary for effective professional practice." National Board Certification candidates for Exceptional Needs certification should take the time to browse here.

National Staff Development Council
http://www.nsdc.org/
The National Staff Development Council (NSDC) is "committed to ensuring success for all students through staff development and school improvement. The Council's fundamental purpose is to address the issues confronted by all participants in the reform process." NSDC provides conferences, publications, and free online resources that can support schools to provide quality staff development. NBCTs who are pursuing new roles in staff development should take the time to browse here.

Association for Supervision and Curriculum Development
http://www.ascd.org/
The Association for Supervision and Curriculum Development (ASCD) "espouses issues of importance to educators; provides a forum in education issues and professionalism; shares research, news, and information; and partners with like-minded organizations and individuals." ASCD has produced numerous award-winning publications. Visit the online "reading room" to access a variety of journals, newsletters, books, and audio- and videotapes including ASCD publications *Educational Leadership*, *The Journal of Curriculum and Supervision*, and *Education Update*.

Electronic School, of the National School Boards Association
http://www.electronic-school.com/
Electronic School is an award-winning technology magazine for K–12 school teachers and administrators that has been created as a free, online

supplement to *American School Board Journal*. It is produced by *ITTE: Education Technology Programs* together with the National School Boards Association. Teachers can access hundreds of articles on issues related to using technology to improve student learning, to improve teacher learning, and to improve the functioning of schools.

American Association of Colleges for Teacher Education
http://www.aacte.org/
The American Association of Colleges for Teacher Education (AACTE) is "a national, voluntary association of colleges and universities with undergraduate or graduate programs to prepare professional educators." A resource for NBCTs looking for new roles in teacher education, the AACTE Web site also provides access to the AACTE Policy Clearinghouse, a resource on education policy at the national, regional, or state level.

Links to National Curriculum Standards

Every state now has its own curriculum standards or learning benchmarks for at least the major subject areas. Some school districts have their own as well. The links below will help you to locate some of the national curriculum standards upon which many regional standards are based. In many cases these online versions are linked to curriculum resources or other related resources. They are all available (at least in part) for free download.

Disagree with some of these standards? Most of these are "living standards" so add your professional opinion to the debate.

Arts:
www.artsedge.kennedy-center.org/professional_resources/standards/nat-standards

English Language Arts:
www.ncte.org/standards/index.shtml

Health:
www.aahperd.org/aahe/template.cfm?template= natl_health_education_standards.html

Math:
www.standards.nctm.org

Music:
www.menc.org/publication/books/prek12st.html

Physical Education:
www.aahperd.org/naspe/publications-nationalstandards.html

Science:
www.nsta.org/onlineresources/nses.asp
www.project2061.org
www.project2061.org/tools/benchol/bolnav.htm
www.project2061.org/tools/sfaaol/sfaatoc.htm

Social Studies/ History:
www.socialstudies.org/standards/toc.html
www.sscnet.ucla.edu/nchs/standards/

Technology:
www.iste.org/standards/

Research Links

We are often confronted with puzzles in the classroom that lead us to wonder, "What does the research say?" Few problems in education have not been encountered by others before. It makes sense to tap into the knowledge base and find out what others before us have learned. A variety of resources are available that can help you to find the answers you need.

If you don't find the answers you need, and even if you do, these Web sites will give you ideas of ways to get involved in conducting and sharing some research of your own.

U.S. Department of Education
http://www.ed.gov/index.jsp

The place to start is the U.S. Department of Education Web site, which can link you to a variety of resources. http://www.ed.gov/index.jsp

The Office of Educational Research and Improvement (OERI) and the major OERI-funded institutions (Centers, Labs, ERIC) have produced a substantial body of educational research and development information which has been made accessible in forms useful beyond the academic research community. But readers must be aware of recent developments that may limit or change access in the future.

According to the American Educational Research Association (AERA), an internal U.S. Department of Education memo from May 31, 2002, recommended the removal of certain content from www.ed.gov, stating, "Content is either outdated or does not reflect the priorities, philosophies, or goals of the present administration."

On November 5, 2002, President Bush signed into law the Education Sciences Reform Act, which dissolved OERI and produced a new organization: the Institute of Education Sciences. According to the U.S. Department of Education Web site, this new organization "reflects the intent of the President and Congress to advance the field of education research, making it more rigorous in support of evidence-based education."

The useful resources listed below which were previously available from OERI is expected to be available in a new archive. Visit http://www.ed.gov/ offices/IES/ for information.

ERIC (Educational Resources Information Center), a project of OERI, has a number of easily accessible and very efficient resources. The homepage is http://eric.ed.gov/. Some of the most useful resources are:

- *A searchable database*—The world's largest source of education information (over 1 million abstracts)
- *AskERIC*—A personalized "reference desk"–style service in which you can browse frequently asked questions or ask your own and get a personalized response.
- Publications for both parents and teachers
- A calendar of education-related conferences (searchable by keyword, sponsor, conference name, date, and location)

OERI has created several collections of **research syntheses**:

- *ERIC Digests*—two-page syntheses of the best, most current research on a topic. http://www.ed.gov/databases/ERIC_Digests/index/
- Research Today is a series of concise research summaries on current topics of national significance. The National Institute on Student Achievement, Curriculum, and Assessment prepares these short reports. http:/ /www.ed.gov/pubs/ResearchToday/
- *Education Consumer Guides* and *Education Research Reports* are two series of publications that were produced within OERI. These publications provide brief, research-based explanations of current concepts and topics. http://www.ed.gov/pubs/OR/ConsumerGuides/ and http:/ /www.ed.gov/pubs/OR/ResearchRpts/
- *CPRE Policy Briefs and Finance Briefs* are 8- to 12-page papers reporting on issues and research in education finance and policy. They are published by the Consortium for Policy Research in Education. http:// www.ed.gov/pubs/CPRE/

There are also **publications, newsletters, and journals** (http:// www.ed. gov/newsletters.html):

- The *Education Statistics Quarterly* was created to make reliable data more accessible. It provides "a quick way to identify information of interest; review key facts, figures, and summary information; and obtain references to detailed data and analyses." By downloading these quarterly publications you can read short publications, summaries, and descriptions of research conducted by the National Center for Education Statistics. http://nces.ed.gov/pubsearch/quarterly

- *The Achiever* is a new electronic newsletter that provides updates on information, events, and announcements about *No Child Left Behind* (April 2002–Present). http://nclb.gov/Newsletter/index.html

- *Community Update*: Each issue features "best practices" and model programs from around the nation on a given topic. Useful summaries of research are provided, such as recent findings by the Public Agenda Foundation on the direction Americans feel education reform should take, as well as references to other resources, services, and relevant publications.

  http://bcol01.ed.gov/CFAPPS/OIIA/communityupdate/page1.cfm

And there are **directories** that you can use to identify further resources:

- *Education Resource Organizations Directory (EROD)*. You can use the Education Resource Organizations Directory to find organizations that provide information and assistance on many education-related topics. You can also utilize the advanced search option to search organizations by the services they provide. http://www.ed.gov/Programs/EROD/

- *Grant and contract information* is available to help you find, apply for, and maintain federal grants.

  http://www.ed.gov/topics/topics.jsp?&top=Grants+%26+Contracts

There are a variety of other nonprofit research links that practitioners will find useful:

Mid-continent Research for Education and Learning
http://www.mcrel.org/
  The Mid-continent Research for Education and Learning (McREL) is "dedicated to improving education for all through applied research, product development, and service." McREL offers field-based research and product development, workshops and training, technical assistance and consulting, evaluation and policy studies, information resources, and community education and public outreach.

Center for Research on Education, Diversity and Excellence
http://www.crede.ucsc.edu/
  Center for Research on Education, Diversity and Excellence (CREDE) is "a federally funded research and development program focused on improving the education of students whose ability to reach their potential is challenged by language or cultural barriers, race, geographic location, or poverty." Through their Web site you can access research findings, learn about CREDE products and projects, and take advantage of links organized by special interest.

National Commission for Teaching and America's Future
http://www.nctaf.org/

The National Commission for Teaching and America's Future (NCTAF) is a great source of information for teachers who are seeking new roles related to teacher preparation, induction, or professional development. This nonpartisan and nonprofit group is "dedicated to improving the quality of teaching nationwide as a means of meeting America's educational challenges."

Other Useful Links: There are hundreds . . . here are just a few

Core Knowledge: www.coreknowledge.org

Rubrics: www.odyssey.on.ca/~elaine.coxon/rubrics.htm

Effective Assessment: www.darkwing.uoregon.edu/~tep/assessment/index.html

Instructional Strategies Glossary: www.glossary.plasmalink.com/glossary

Scaffold Instruction: www.magnet.sandi.net/overview/scaffold.html

Graphic Organizers: www.graphic.org/goindex.html

Pathway to School Improvement (Curriculum, Instruction, and so on): www.ncrel.org/sdrs

Multiple Intelligences: www.mcmel.org/erica.mi/mainpage.html

Play: www.playfuladventures.com/links.htm

Literacy: www.ed.uri.edu/smart/homepage/lithp.htm

Special Education: www.utm.edu/~annetter/sped

Looking at Student Work protocols: www.lasw.org

National Writing Project: www.writingproject.org

Links to e-mail communities

This book argues that teachers experience a more fulfilling personal and professional growth experience from National Board Certification when they work together in groups. Knowing that this is true, thousands of teachers across the country have found creative ways to connect themselves via the Web.

Candidates should note that these e-mail communities are not moderated or officially endorsed by the NBPTS. Any information or advice received from these groups should be taken as unofficial. Authoritative information is provided on the National Board's Web site.

NBCTs who participate in e-mail communities should note that there are guidelines from the National Board on working with candidates and establishing networks. Download the *Handbook for National Board Certified Teachers* at http://www.nbpts.org/pdf/nbcts_handbook_2001.pdf.

Yahoo Groups

The "Yahoo Groups" is the largest e-mail community network and it has a different section for each certificate area. Some groups are more active than others, and each provides different levels of intellectual, emotional, and logistical support. You can obtain information on how to join by following the appropriate link below. If you want to learn about other groups you might talk to local NBCTs.

All begin with <www.groups.yahoo.com/group>.
For example: Early Adolescent/Young Adult Art is:
www.groups.yahoo.com/group/eaya-art

Early Adolescent/Young Adult Art:	/eaya-art
Elementary/Middle Art:	/emcart
Career and Technical Ed (CTE):	/nbptscareerteched
Adol./Young Adult–English Lang.:	/aya-ela
Early Adol.-English Language Arts:	/eaela
English:	/nbpts-english
English New Language-ENL:	/nbpts_enl
Exceptional Needs:	/exceptional-needs
Early Adolescent Generalist:	/NBPTS-EA-GEN
Early Childhood Generalist:	/ec_gen
Library Media:	/librarymedia
Middle Childhood Generalist-NBC:	/MC-GEN-NBC
Middle Childhood Generalist-NBCII:	/MC_GEN_NBC_II
Middle Childhood Generalist:	/mcgenonly
Adolescent/Young Adult Math:	/ayamath
Early Adolescent Math:	/ea_math
Music:	/NBPTSmusic
Early/Middle Music:	/musicmc
Physical Education:	/nbpts-phys-educ
Early Adolescent Science:	/EASCI
Adolescent/Adult Science:	/nbpts-adoladult-sci
Adol./Young Adult Social Studies:	/nbpts-ayasocialstudies
Early Adolescent Social Studies:	/eass
Vocational:	/vocational
ForeignLanguage/World Languages:	/NBPTSFL
Career/Technical Education:	/NBPTScareerteched

NBCT Discussion Forums

The NBPTS Web site has a section designated for National Board Certified Teachers which provides access to password-protected discussion forums. These forums were established to create "collegial discourse and resource sharing without the constraints of geography," and they currently exist in four areas: research, mentoring, teacher leadership, and candidate support. NBCTs who are seeking new roles will benefit from the expertise of others that are engaged in similar work. You can access them directly at http://www.nbpts.org/events/discus.cfm.

Links to the National Board

The only authoritative source for logistical help is the National Board for Professional Teaching Standards. The NBPTS Web site is easy to navigate and very comprehensive. Bookmark this link and visit this site first with any question you have: www.nbpts.org.

Frequently Asked Questions

Candidates can find answers to most of their questions regarding the National Board process on the "Frequently Asked Questions" page of the National Board's Web site. Questions about the certification requirements and process which are not answered on the Web site must be submitted in writing. They can easily be submitted via the Web site, but are also accepted via U.S. mail and fax.
http://www.mserv2.net/nis/inquiry-home-action.do?versionID=3&go=OK

Immediate Response

If you have questions about portfolios, assessment centers, scoring, or other related issues and need an immediate response (and you have already tried the Web site), try calling **1-800-22TEACH.** This resource is available 8:00 AM - 6:00 PM (CST) Monday through Friday (excluding holidays). Be prepared with your certificate and your candidate ID number when you call. Be prepared for the fact that they may not be able to answer your questions; they may refer you to the FAQ section of the Web site and/or ask you to put your question in writing.

NBPTS Offices

The National Board for Professional Teaching Standards has several offices:

The National Office in Arlington
1525 Wilson Boulevard, Suite 500
Arlington, VA 22209
(703) 465-2700

This is the home office. The president of NBPTS keeps an office here. It also includes the divisions for certification standards, marketing, communication, and public relations.

The San Antonio Office
19500 Bulverde Road
San Antonio, TX 78259-3701
1(800)22-TEACH

This office managed by Harcourt/The Psychological Corporation handles **all logistics related to the certification process** and forwards requests for National Board publications to its Fulfillment Division. This is the only office candidates will have reason to contact.

Southfield Office
26555 Evergreen Rd
Suite 400
Southfield, MI 48076
(248) 351-4444

This was the original home office. It now includes the divisions for assessment development, finance, NBCT opportunities, higher education and teacher development, and human resources.

Regional Offices
The National Board also has several regional offices that can help connect candidates, NBCTs, and the public to resources they need. Find them through the National Board's Web site.
http://www.nbpts.org/about/dept.cfm

Bibliography

American Federation of Teachers. "Principles for Professional Development." Washington, D.C.: American Federation of Teachers, 1995.

Blythe, Tina, David Allen, and Barbara S. Powell. *Looking Together at Students' Work: A Companion Guide to Assessing Student Learning.* New York: Teachers' College Press, 1999.

Bond, Lloyd, Tracy W. Smith, Wanda K. Baker, and John A. Hattie. "The Certification System of the National Board for Professional Teaching Standards: A Construct and Consequential Validity Study." Greensboro, North Carolina: University of North Carolina at Greensboro, 2000.

Bransford, John D., Ann L. Brown, and Rodney R. Cocking, eds. *How People Learn: Brain, Mind, Experience and School.* Edited by Commission on Behavioral and Social Sciences and Education and National Research Council. Expanded Edition ed. Washington, D.C.: National Academy Press, 2000.

Bredeson, Paul, Marvin Firth, and Katherine Kasten. "Organizational Incentives and Secondary School Teaching." *Journal of Research and Development in Education* 16, no. 4 (1983): 52-58.

Brophy, J. "How Teachers Influence What is Taught and Learned in Classrooms," *The Elementary School Journal* 83, no.1 (1982):1-13.

Cohen, David. "Teaching Practice: Plus que ca change." In *Contributing to Educational Change*, edited by P. W. Jackson, 27-84. Berkeley, CA: McCrutcham Publishing Corporation, 1988.

Cohen, David, and Deborah Lowenberg Ball. "Instruction, Capacity and Improvement." Consortium for Policy Research in Education, 1999.

Coleman, James S. , E.Q. Campbell, C.J. Hobson, J. McPartland, Mood A.M., F.D. Weinfeld, and R.L. York. "Equality of Educational Opportunity." 33. Washington, D.C.: National Center for Educational Statistics (DHEW), 1966.

Cranton, Patricia. *Professional Development as Transformational Learning.* San Francisco: Jossey-Bass, 1996.

Cushman, Kathleen. "Looking Collaboratively at Student Work: An Essential Toolkit." *Horace*, November 1996.

Darling-Hammond, Linda. "What Matters Most: Teaching for America's Future." New York: National Commission on Teaching and America's Future, 1996.

Darling-Hammond, Linda and Gary Sykes, eds. *Teaching as the Learning Profession.* San Francisco: Jossey-Bass, 1999.

Duckworth, Eleanor. *"The Having of Wonderful Ideas" and Other Essays on Teaching and Learning*. New York: Teachers College Press, 1987.

Elmore, Richard. "The Role of Local School Districts in Instructional Improvement," in *Designing Coherent Policy*, edited by S. Fuhrman. San Francisco: Jossey-Bass, 1993.

————. *Building a New Structure for School Leadership*. Washington D.C.: Albert Shanker Institute, 2000.

————. "Professional Development and the Practice of Large-Scale Improvement." Paper prepared for the Albert Shanker Institute. Washington, D.C., 2002.

Evans, Robert. "The Culture of Resistance." In *The Jossey-Bass Reader on School Reform*, 510-21. San Francisco: Jossey-Bass, 2001.

Fullan, Michael. *The New Meaning of Education Reform*. New York: Teachers' College Press, 2001.

Garet, Michael, Andrew Porter, Laura Desimone, Beatrice F. Birman, and Kwang Suk Yoon. "What Makes Professional Development Effective? Results from a National Sample of Teachers." *American Educational Research Journal* 38, no. 4 (2001): 915-45.

Gusky, Thomas R. "Attitude and Perceptual Change in Teachers." *International Journal of Educational Research* 13, no. 4 (1989): 439-453.

Hawkins, David. "I, Thou and It." In *The Informed Vision: Essays on Learning and Human Nature*, edited by David Hawkins, 49-62. New York: Agathon Books, 1974.

Hawley, W. & Valli, L. "The Essentials of Professional Development: A New Consensus." In *Teaching as the Learning Profession: Handbook of Policy and Practice*, edited by G. Sykes & L. Darling-Hammond. San Francisco: Jossey-Bass, 1999.

Huberman, Michael. "Networks That Alter Teaching: Conceptualizations, Exchanges, and Experiments." *Teachers and Teaching: Theory and Practice* 1995, 193-211.

Hussar, W. J. *Predicting the Need for Newly Hired Teachers in the United States to 2008-9*. Washington, D.C.: National Center for Education Statistics, 1999.

Ingersoll, Richard M. "A Different Approach to Solving the Teacher Shortage Problem." *Teaching Quality: Policy Briefs*, no. 3 (2001): 1-7.

Jencks, C., and M. Phillips. "The Black-White Test Score Gap: An Introduction." In *The Black-White Test Score Gap*, edited by C. Jencks, Phillips, M., 1-51. Washington, D.C.: Brookings Institution Press, 1991.

Johnson, Susan Moore. "Can Professional Certification for Teachers Reshape Teaching as a Career?' *Phi Delta Kappan* 82, no.5 (January, 2001): 393-399.

Kardos, Susan, Susan Moore Johnson, Heather G. Peske, David Kauffman, and Edward Liu. "Counting on Colleagues: New Teachers Encounter the Professional Cultures of their Schools." *Educational Administration Quarterly* 37, no.2 (2001): 250-290.

Kegan, Robert, and Lisa Laskow Lahey. *How the Way We Talk Can Change the Way We Work.* San Francisco: Jossey-Bass, 2001.

Lagemann, Ellen Condliffe. *The Elusive Science: The Troubling History of Education Research.* Chicago: The University of Chicago Press, 2000.

Lewis, Anne C. "A New Consensus Emerges on the Characteristics of Good Professional Development." *Harvard Education Letter,* May/June 1997, 1-4.

Little, Judith Warren. "Norms of Collegiality and Experimentation: Workplace Conditions of School Success." *American Educational Research Journal* 19, no. 3 (1982): 325-40.

————. "Assessing the Prospects for Teacher Leadership." In *Building a Professional Culture in Schools,* edited by A. Lieberman, 78-106. New York: Teachers College Press, 1988.

————. "The Persistence of Privacy: Autonomy and Initiative in Teachers' Professional Relations." *Teachers College Record* 91, no. 4 (1990): 509-36.

Lortie, Dan C. *Schoolteacher: A Sociological Study.* Chicago: The University of Chicago Press, 1975.

McMillan, James H., and Daisy F. Reed. "At-Risk Students and Resiliency: Factors Contributing to Academic Success." *The Clearing House* 67 (1994): 137-40.

Meier, Deborah. *In Schools We Trust.* Boston: Beacon Press, 2002.

Murnane, Richard J., and Frank Levy. *Teaching the New Basic Skills: Principles for Educating Children to Thrive in a Changing Economy.* New York: The Free Press, 1996.

National Alliance of Business. "Investing in Teaching." Washington, DC: National Alliance of Business, 2001.

National Board for Professional Teaching Standards. "What Teachers Should Know and Be Able to Do." Southfield, MI: National Board for Professional Teaching Standards, 1999.

————."I Am a Better Teacher." Southfield, MI: National Board for Professional Teaching Standards, 2001.

————. "The Impact of National Board Certification on Teachers: A Survey of National Board Certified Teachers and Assessors." Southfield, MI: National Board for Professional Teaching Standards, 2001.

National Center for Education Statistics. *NCES Digest of Education Statistics* [website]. 2000 cited. Available from nces.ed.gov/pubs2001/digest.

National Commission on Excellence in Education. "A Nation at Risk: The Imperative for Educational Reform." Washington, D.C., 1983.

National Research Council, Committee on a Strategic Education Research Partnership. "A Strategic Education Research Partnership to Bridge Research and Practice." Edited by A.K. Wigdor, M.S. Donovan, and C.E. Snow. Division of Behavioral and Social Sciences and Education. Washington, D.C.: The National Academies Press, (2002).

Nemser, Sharon Feiman. *Learning to Teach.* New York: Longman, 1983.

OERI. *TIMSS: More About the Project* U.S. Department of Education, 2002 [cited 2002]. Available from http://nces.ed.gov/timss/timss95/index.asp.

Peske, Heather G., Ed Liu, Susan Moore Johnson, David Kauffman, and Susan M. Kardos. "The Next Generation of Teachers: Changing Conceptions of a Career in Teaching." *Phi Delta Kappa*, December 2001, 304-11.

Ravitch, Diane. "National Standards in American Education: A Citizen's Guide." Washington, D.C.: Brookings Institution, 1995.

Rosenholtz, Susan, Otto Bassler, and Kathy Hoover-Dempsey. "Organizational Conditions of Teacher Learning." *Teaching and Teacher Education* 2, no. 2 (1986): 91-104.

Sagor, Richard. *Guiding School Improvement with Action Research*. Alexandria, VA: Association for Supervision and Curriculum Development, 2000.

Sanders, William L., and June C. Rivers. "Cumulative and Residual Effects of Teachers on Future Student Academic Achievement." Knoxville, TN: University of Tennessee Value-Added Research and Assessment Center, 1996.

Saphier, Jonathan D., and M. King. "Good Seeds Grow in Strong Cultures." *Educational Leadership* 42 (1985): 67-73.

Saphier, Jonathan D. *Bonfires and Magic Bullets: Making Teaching a True Profession, the Step Without which Other Reforms Will Neither Take nor Endure*. Carlisle, MA: Research for Better Teaching, 1995.

Schein, Edgar H. *Organizational Culture and Leadership, Jossey-Bass Management Series*. San Francisco: Jossey-Bass, 1992.

Schlechty, Phillip C. *Schools for the 21st Century: Leadership Imperatives for Educational Reform*. San Francisco: Jossey-Bass, 1990.

Shavelson, Richard J., and Lisa Towne, eds. *Scientific Research in Education*. Edited by National Research Council, *Committee on Scientific Principles in Education*. Washington D.C.: National Academy Press, 2002.

Shulman, L. and Gary Sykes, eds. *Handbook of Teaching and Policy*. New York: Longman, 1983.

Sparks, Dennis, and Steven Hirsh. "A New Vision for Staff Development." National Staff Development Council (NSDC) and Association for Supervision and Curriculum Development (ASCD), 1997.

Thomas B. Fordham Foundation. "The Teachers We Need and How to Get More of Them: A Manifesto." In *Better Teachers, Better Schools*, edited by M. Kanstoroom and Jr. Chester Finn. Washington, D.C.: Thomas B. Fordham Foundation, 1999.

Tucker, Mark S., and Judy B. Codding. "Setting High Standards for Everyone." In *Standards for Our Schools: How to Set Them, Measure Them, and Reach Them*. San Francisco: Jossey-Bass, 1988.

Tyack, David, and Larry Cuban. *Tinkering Toward Utopia: A Century of Public School Reform*. Cambridge: Harvard University Press, 1995.

Wenger, Etienne. *Communities of Practice: Learning Meaning and Identity*. New York: Cambridge University Press, 1998.

Index

About the Author

Jill Harrison Berg is a National Board Certified Teacher on sabbatical from Cambridge Public Schools' Cambridgeport School while serving as a doctoral fellow at Harvard University Graduate School of Education. She is a recipient of the Roy E. Larsen Fellowship as well as the James Bryant Conant Fellowship. Her research interest is improving teacher practice and student learning through reflection. Her work in teacher education extends from facilitating workshops with preservice teachers, to consulting with school teams about using data to inform instruction, to presenting workshops at local and national conferences, to supporting teacher candidates for National Board Certification. She is committed to supporting work that recognizes the importance of the practitioner's perspective in developing educational endeavors. She has collaborated or consulted on special projects within a variety of organizations including the National Research Council, RAND, Interstate New Teacher Assessment and Support Consortium (INTASC), Project Zero, WGBH, UNICEF, TERC Investigations, and the Massachusetts Department of Education. She earned her master's degree from Lesley University through the Shady Hill School Teacher Training Course and her bachelor's degree from Harvard University. She is a member of the Bahá'í Faith, and she lives in Boston with her husband and two children.

Contributing NBCTs

Twelve additional National Board Certified Teachers were contributing authors for the activities in the "Tookit for Candidate Groups" included in this book. All of these accomplished teachers are working in public schools in urban, suburban, or rural Massachusetts. Through their National Board Certification and their commitment to mentoring others within the profession, they have each earned the designation of Master Teacher in Massachusetts. Together they have over 200 years of teaching experience, have supported the growth of over 600 student teachers and teachers who are new to the profession, and have guided over 300 candidates through the process of National Board Certification.

Jane Beane has been teaching Kindergarten through Grade 3 in Lawrence for 30 years. She is a mentor for Lawrence Public School teachers and conducts workshops for math and developmentally appropriate practices. She is also a member of the Massachusetts Leadership Academy. She is currently working with the Massachusetts Department of Education on a Kindergarten Science curriculum with Min-hua Chen. She has a C.A.G.S. degree from Fitchburg State College.

Dr. **Al Bird** is an educator of long standing, having been at the chalkboard in front of a class for the first time teaching sailing theory when he was only15 years old. He has taught at every level from kindergarten student through doctoral students, and holds degrees in Math, Physics, Nuclear Engineering, Operations Management, and Finance.

Martha Bosco has spent most of her 30-year professional career teaching in the primary grades. In addition to her classroom experiences she has taught graduate-level courses on educational strategies. She holds masters degrees in both Elementary Special Education and Elementary School Administration. She is a member of the Massachusetts Leadership Academy, Delta Kappa Gamma, and Phi Lambda Theta.

Judith Cournoyer has 21 years experience as a regular and special education teacher. She received the Robert W. Haynes Foundation Award for Excellence in 2000. She is a member of the Massachusetts Teacher Leadership Academy and Delta Kappa Gamma. She has presented workshops and taught graduate courses on multifaceted reading instruction.

Dr. Matthew Delaney, (Ed.D.) has been active in NBPTS candidate support and educational leadership; has broad experience in art, media, and technology including International Conference on Internet & Society/Harvard Law School (two scholarships), NBPTS, NAEA, New England Art Education Association, and has done extensive photography, writing, design, and illustration for regional, national, and international educational and corporate sectors.

Jim Dixon has 12 years of teaching experience at Dennis-Yarmouth Regional High School and Silver Lake Regional High School. He has taught at Northeastern University and is currently an adjunct faculty member at Stonehill College teaching courses in Assessment and helping to recreate their secondary education program using National Board standards. He holds a master's degree in Biology from SUNY at Buffalo and a bachelor's degree from Fordham University.

Mary Guerino teaches second grade in Foxborough, Massachusetts. She was a caseworker for the Department of Youth Services in Massachusetts for 5 years before becoming a stay-at-home mom for 13 years. For the past 10 years she has been teaching first and second grade. She is a member of the district's Staff Development Team. She mentors National Board Candidates as well as new teachers. She has presented regional workshops in math and science and national workshops on writing.

Dr. Kevin Hart (J.D., Ph.D. History) taught at Seattle University and Kansas State University and served as an Army Judge Advocate before retiring in 1995. Since then he has taught history and acted as department team leader at Oakmont Regional High School and, since 1997 he has served as the social studies coordinator for the Ashburnham-Westminster Regional School District.

Paul Lyness has been a mathematics teacher at Marblehead High School for the past 34 years. He has co-authored a workbook on the N.Y. Regents High School math exam. He was a consultant on two other workbooks on the Florida Comprehensive Aptitude test in mathematics at the 8th- and 10th-grade levels.

Prior to teaching, **Elizabeth Sales** was an executive editor in the school division of Houghton Mifflin Company. For the past 15 years she has been teaching, most recently math at the middle-school level. She is a member of many committees in the district—a few include a site-based student assistance team, district mentor steering committee, math task force and leadership planning committee.

Carol Shestok is the K to 5 Science and Mentor Training Coordinator in Westford, Massachusetts. She has taught elementary school for 21 years. She presents nationally/internationally, teaches graduate courses, and has published in college texts as well as state and national periodicals. She is a Presidential Award winner for Excellence in Science, a Massachusetts Teacher of Year Finalist (2000), and a recipient of the EPA/MA Environmental Excellence award. She is currently a doctoral candidate at the University of Massachusetts in Lowell.

 **Anne Stacy** has been teaching first grade for 22 years. She helped design and establish a mentoring program in her district of Ashland, Massachusetts, and is presently one of the coordinators. She has mentored NBPTS candidates for 4 years. She feels she is constantly reflecting on her practice as a result of the high standards firmly implanted in her by the NBPTS.

About the Illustrators

All illustrations are the original work of Althea Zemnaan Berg and Summer Lee Martin Payton, accomplished artists who have been drawing for five years. They are both 6 years old and in the first grade.